Walking in Favor:

A Journey of Faith, Perseverance, and Love

by

Bernice M. Pitts

Walking in Favor: A Journey of Faith, Perseverance, and Love. Copyright 2024 by Linda Cooks. All rights reserved. No part of this publication may be reproduced, distributed, or transmitted in any form or by any means, including photocopying, recording, or other electronic or mechanical methods, without the prior written permission of the author or publisher, except in the case of brief quotations embodied in critical reviews and certain other noncommercial uses as permitted by U.S. copyright law.

For permission requests, contact Linda Cooks at lcooks7232@gmail.com. Silver Bangles Productions books may be purchased for educational, business, or sales promotional use at www.silverbanglesproductions.com. For more information please email info@silverbanglesproductions.com.

Book Cover by Linda Cooks and Panagiotis Lampridis

Images provided by the Pitts family

Printed in the U.S.A.

First printing, January 2024

Library of Congress Control Number: 2024901128

ISBN: 979-8-9888463-1-4

I found that that's the best attitude you can have when facing blatant racism…a positive attitude and persistence.

– Bernice M. Pitts

I am very grateful, thankful, and blessed to dedicate this book to my parents Mack and Lena Carr, my husband Carroll Pitts, Jr., my two children Philip and Pamela, my play daughter Cynthia Pressley, and my grandson Jerrai. I also dedicate this book to my loving church family and many friends. To God be the glory!

Contents

Introduction	9
Chapter 1 : My Childhood	12
Chapter 2 : Spreading the Gospel	19
Chapter 3 : California, Here I Come	24
Chapter 4 : A New Home	27
Chapter 5 : Stepping Out on Faith	35
Chapter 6 : Establishing New Roots	52
Chapter 7 : Journeys to New Lands	59
Chapter 8 : Loss of Loved Ones	65
Chapter 9 : Keep on Living	70
Chapter 10 : Life Now - What's Next	75
Chapter 11: Stepping Out Again	78
Epilogue	87
Love Letters from Carroll Pitts, Jr. to Bernice Maxine Pitts	90
About the Joint Author	98

Dear Reader,

I sincerely thank you for your interest in my book! I had never thought about writing a book, but when I shared one of my life experiences with my church family and friends, many of them suggested that I should write a book of my life stories.

Two of my young church sisters later came to me and said if I shared my story with them they would write it and get it ready for publication. I agreed. We got started in 2021 and it's been an almost three-year journey.

My book will enlighten you about the stages of my life from childhood, college at Pepperdine as a student and a wife, accepting my role as a minister's wife, and then becoming a mother. When I became a young woman, I was on a mission to choose my husband and I did. Later he and I adopted two children, both of whom are now deceased. I became a widow after 40 years of marriage. I celebrated my 75th, 80th, 85th, 90th, and 95th birthdays fabulously with church family and friends. I am comfortably living alone and I continued to drive until very recently. I've had a wonderful and blessed life. To God be the glory.

As interesting as these facts may be, my book gets into much more than this. I hope you enjoy reading my book about my life as much as I have enjoyed living my life.

Gratefully,

Bernice M. Pitts

Introduction

written by Linda Cooks

A few years ago in 2018 I was sitting in my parents' kitchen on a Saturday afternoon in Los Angeles enjoying a visit with Sis. Bernice Pitts. At 90 years old, she drove to our house for lunch among her day of activities. She was sharing a story from her childhood. Sis. Pitts is a natural raconteur. Her upright posture, cadence of speech, and knowing smile make it clear that she's skilled at captivating an audience. And captivated I was. The story of her childhood in Oklahoma and what led her to move to California was all new to me, and I found it both fascinating and inspirational. How had I gone all these years without hearing this narrative of her life that she shared so freely with others?

I had known Sis. Pitts since I was a child, but never spent time with her in a small, casual setting. My parents were baptized into Christ and joined the Normandie Church of Christ congregation in Los Angeles when I was five years old. They said that I started to ask them questions about who God was, who made the sky blue, and other inquiries they felt would be better addressed in a church setting. I came to know Sis. Pitts as the wife of the church's minister, Bro. Carroll Pitts. As many folks do, she sits in a favored pew. Her's is near the front on the right side of the church. Her Sunday attire is always a colorful, monochromatic ensemble, matching from a stylish hat to dressy shoes. Her soprano voice during our lively congregational singing set the standard for the high register of notes I tried to reach. I enjoyed singing, but I wouldn't brand my voice as one created to entertain others. This was confirmed at a church conference banquet in Atlanta in 1997. Several friends and I voluntarily participated in the evening's entertainment by forming an impromptu group and singing a song that we all knew, but did not take the time to practice together. I didn't think we sounded that bad, but to our surprise (and embarrassment), members of the audience began to clink their glasses with silverware and boo us from the stage! So much for making a joyful noise unto the Lord. We stopped singing and walked back to our dinner table. The emcee for the evening's program walked to the podium we just left and shamed the audience for their rude behavior. To my dismay, she insisted that our singing group come back to the stage and resume our performance! Well there was no way we were going back on that stage; we stayed planted in our seats. After a few awkward moments I saw Sis. Pitts, head held high, walk to the front of the room with a sheet of paper in hand. The emcee stood aside as she reached the microphone and recited a lovely and entertaining poem, "Heaven's Grocery Store." The audience was ecstatic! They gave her a roaring round of applause. Members of our table gave her a standing ovation. I would say we couldn't believe how she was able to turn the night around, but that was Sis. Pitts. She's still the same confident, motivating woman today.

 Years later as I listened to and laughed with Sis. Pitts that afternoon in my parents' home, I imagined that others would enjoy her stories as much as I have. I decided to ask her if she ever considered writing her life story. I offered to help her with the process of developing her story into a book. After prodding from close friends and a stark curtailing of her usual excursions during the COVID-19 pandemic, Sis. Pitts agreed to begin the process of writing her biography. It has been an honor to share this experience with her. The context of my adolescent reminiscences has expanded to include sisterly conversations between two adult friends.

An appreciation of God's blessings as well an enduring spiritual strength has been her stance throughout life. With candor and a sense of humor, Sis. Pitts shares poignant moments in her life that reflect her firm belief in God's promises, even from a young age. *"For I know the plans I have for your life," declares the Lord, "plans to prosper you and not to harm you, plans to give you hope and a future." Jeremiah 29:11.* It is my hope that readers find her optimistic outlook on life, fervor for adventure, and faith in God as inspirational as I have.

Chapter 1

My Childhood

It was a beautiful day in Los Angeles in December 2021. The kind of sunny, winter day that convinced visitors of the city to make L.A. their home. I arrived at Sis. Pitts' house with my laptop and recorder. As always she greeted me with a warm smile and welcoming spirit. We sat down at the dining room table. To my surprise, she handed me 12 handwritten pages of her life story! I grinned as I realized that she was just as excited to share her story as I was to hear it. I asked her to read her story into my recorder. Sis. Pitts has always had a way of making words on paper come alive with her vocal tones and word accentuation. I knew I was in for a treat.

I am Bernice Pitts and I am 95 years old at this time. I'm the only child born to Mack and Lena Carr. I was born in Okmulgee, Oklahoma May 21st, 1928. I have had a long life, which I have enjoyed. I have had my ups and downs, but God has been with me all these years. I have shared my life with many people and some have told me that I should write a book. Should I be able to complete this task, I hope and pray that generations to come may read and be encouraged and inspired to strive to obey our heavenly Father in order to be able to spend eternal life in heaven.

I will begin with my early childhood which began in 1928 in Okmulgee, Oklahoma.[1] I remember living on the outskirts of Okmulgee. We were not on a farm, but we did have a cow and chickens. I remember having a fighting rooster who was exactly that, a fighter. At that time we had an outhouse, if you have ever even heard of that. When I would have to go to the outhouse, I would have a stick with me to fight the rooster. I always remembered to take my stick. Sometimes when my mom went to the outhouse she would have a stick too and she could hit harder than me. I remember once or twice she knocked out the rooster. Then she hollered to us to put on the water because we were going to have the rooster for dinner. Just like that, he would come to and get up and run away before he got into *more* trouble!

When I reached five years old my mother decided not to enroll me in kindergarten because the school in the country was about three miles away and she thought that it was too far for me to walk. Just so you know, I passed a White school on the way to my Black school. So my mother kept me home and taught me herself. She taught me my ABC's forward and backwards. I still recite them for children these days. After that I attended the country school for 1st and 2nd grade and then later we moved to the city where I attended 3rd and 4th grades.

Around this same time, I met a dear friend named Catherine Marks. She was one year older than me but one grade below me. We had a great time at school playing jacks. They said I was a champion jack player, but Catherine never went out without a fight. When Catherine was in the 3rd and I was in the 4th grade, her

---

1 Okmulgee is located over 30 miles south of Tulsa and was founded just after the Civil War in 1868. It is the capital of the Muscogee (Creek) Nation. With nearby rivers and springs, the community was named, oki mulgee, meaning "boiling waters." Bamburg, Maxine, "Okmulgee." *The Encyclopedia of Oklahoma History and Culture.*

parents moved to Phoenix, Arizona. I surely was sad when she left, but fortunately we were able to keep in touch by mail. I enjoyed being penpals with Cat. Thankfully, all these years later we are still good friends and sisters in Christ right now. I am 95 and she is 96.

Growing up as a child things were going well at school, but not so much at home. Something was happening with my parents. They were not getting along very well and my mother was tired of the way my dad was acting. He would just run around with his buddies and stay out all night. In his defense, there wasn't that much to do in Ocmulgee. The men would go down to 5th Street (that was the Black street in the city) and they would just stick together and talk and maybe drink for hours. I don't know whether they were running women or not, but my mother probably suspected they were. Eventually she got fed up with that. She wrote to her older sister, my Auntie Josie, who, ironically, also lived in Phoenix, Arizona. Now, just to help you understand, my mother comes from a family of 11 girls and 5 boys, and she was next to the baby of that big group. This sister that was in Arizona was like a mother to her because my mother's mother died when she was only 8 years old. Her older sisters pretty much finished raising her. So when my mother wrote my aunt out in Arizona and said that she had had about all that she could take from Mack, my dad, saying, "He won't change. I'm just tired. I have a choice to make. I either have to leave him or kill him." My aunt quickly advised my mom, "Please don't kill him, but do tell him that *he* has a decision to make. Tell him that you and Bernice are coming to see me. He can come too or he can stay there."

My mom took her sister's advice and she began getting her things and my things together for our trip. When she told my dad, he didn't believe her until she started packing. When he realized that my mom was serious, he started getting his things together too. A few days later we started loading up our car. We owned a 1928 Chevrolet. The car and I were the same age. When we were ready to leave, my dad put a $10 bill in his pocket to see how far it would take us. When we reached my aunt's house, he had a nickel left. Back then, gas was about $0.10 per gallon.

We were able to stay with my aunt for a while. My dad was acting very well now. I guess it was a blessing when we left Oklahoma. There was no one to get in trouble with. He stayed home with the family. My aunt introduced him to some of her friends who helped him get a job. The first job he got was in Buckeye, Arizona about 35 miles from Phoenix. He was working at a cotton gin making $25 per week! We thought we had struck it rich. I used to have fun running on top of the bales of cotton. My mom got a job working for a White lady. We did quite well and a few months later, we went back to Oklahoma on vacation. We had purchased a 1936 Chevy to drive back. It was a shiny black one. My grandparents and friends thought we had struck it rich in Arizona as well.

In Buckeye I attended a one-room building for K through 6th grade taught by one teacher. At this time I was in the 5th grade. After about two years, my dad got a job in Phoenix. He was to start before school was out. I think it was about four months before the school year was ending. He told me that once he started his new job I would have to go to school in Phoenix. I cried because I did not want to change schools. I had already gotten used to my school in Buckeye and I loved my teacher. She would let me take the little ones outside to play and teach them songs. I had a good friend named Bernice Palmer who was in my class. We decided to work together to get our parents to agree to let me stay in Buckeye to finish 6th grade; I would stay with Bernice and her family. The Palmer family had a lot of children. I hoped that one more would not matter too much.

Well it worked, and our parents agreed. To make matters even better, my teacher would go to Phoenix on weekends so my mom asked her to bring me when my parents could not come get me. One weekend before Easter, I rode into Phoenix with my teacher and I came back to Buckeye on Saturday evening. On Easter Sunday, one of the Palmer boys drove us to church and he was racing with someone on dirt roads. The driver lost control and turned the car over. He was driving a big Studebaker. There were six or seven children in the car. I think the car had a top that was not steel and several children went flying out the top. I think the driver of the car had the car on his neck and I was still in the car. I remember crying because I had messed up my new Easter dress, lost one shoe, and had a scar on my forehead that had to be closed. I don't think the doctors stitched up my skin though, they were more like clamps to hold the scar together. Suffice it to say that after that event, I was looking forward to going to my parents' place.

Once I moved back home with my parents in Phoenix, Catherine and I would visit one another. Sometimes I would stay over the weekend and her mother would shampoo our hair. She would braid mine and press Cat's. I remember one day crying about this because she wouldn't press mine. She tried to make me understand that my hair didn't need pressing, but it didn't matter, I kept on crying. Then Cat's mom took us shopping to buy us new pajamas and I started crying again because I could not fit the pj's that Cat could wear. I had to get mine in the teenage section. I was large for my age and Cat was small. In fact, my mom said I weighed 10 lbs. at birth. Sometimes when we would go to the movies, I would have to wait to let Cat buy the tickets because they wanted me to pay full price. I was only 10 or 11 and Cat was either 11 or 12. I couldn't stand it. I was so happy when I reached 13 and finally looked my age.

After I moved to Phoenix with my parents, I checked into my new school as a 7th grader. I really enjoyed my new school and the school year went by fast. We were approaching summer vacation when my uncle shared some town news with my dad. He told him that there was a tent gospel meeting going on not far from our house. The church holding the meeting had a tract printed that they were passing out to visitors promising them a $100 reward if they could find certain scriptures in the bible. My dad could hardly wait to go to the meeting.

The first night we walked to the meeting and picked up a tract. The tract required the reader to find bible scriptures that supported commonly held beliefs about Christianity. My dad called our Baptist preacher and asked him to help him find the scriptures and to go with us to the meeting. The next night, our Baptist preacher came with us to see the visiting preacher at the tent meeting, a man named Levi Kennedy from a Church of Christ congregation in Chicago. As we sat in our seats listening to him, we realized that this man was truly preaching the Bible. After the meeting, my family and our Baptist preacher started walking back home and my dad asked the preacher to stop by the house to help him find bible scriptures that specifically described the Baptist Church and some of its practices. First, the preacher asked my dad to bring the dictionary.

My dad said, "Levi Kennedy did not mention a dictionary."

Then the preacher said, "Well I guess it's not in the Bible, but that's just what we do in the Baptist church."

When my dad realized that the Baptist church he had been attending was not based on biblical teaching, he said, "I'm getting out of this."

"No, you don't need to do that. We're ok too. God still recognizes our church."

"No, we're not ok if it's not in the Bible," my dad said. "We are going back tomorrow night to be baptized into the Church of Christ."

"If I lose the Carr family (that's us), I may as well go back to the world."[2]

My dad told him that he's already in the world. He had better come go with us.

Well, we went that third night and we were baptized. Bro. Kennedy was so happy. I can't remember whether or not that was the last night of the meeting, but later that night my dad said to me, "On Monday morning, tell your teacher to give you your report card because we have to go back to Oklahoma."

I obeyed him and that Monday I asked for my report card and the teacher gave it to me. I was passing on to the 8th grade. I was so happy to learn that before my classmates learned theirs.

When I got home from school, I said to my dad, "We only have a week to go to school. Can't we wait until next week is over?"

My dad said, "No, we can't wait." I didn't understand why then, but I later realized that after learning about the gospel, he realized the urgency of sharing the good news of salvation with our family and loved ones back in Oklahoma. He was determined to spread the word and to do so immediately.

---

2   "Go back to the world" means backsliding into a lifestyle where you are not committed to the teachings of Christ. I John 2:15-16: Do not love the world or anything in the world. If anyone loves the world, love for the Father is not in them. For everything in the world–the lust of the flesh, the lust of the eyes, and the pride of life–comes not from the Father but from the world.

Chapter 2

Spreading the Gospel

Tulsa was a lot different from Okulmgee. In the early 1900s, North Tulsa was known as Black Wall Street. It was a thriving town of professional offices, movie theaters, a bank, library, post office, schools, clothing stores, restaurants, and other Black businesses. This commercial district known as Deep Greenwood serviced Black residents who were banned by segregation laws from shopping in White neighborhoods. In 1921 however, the community was devastated by a massacre of racial violence sparked by White mobs that were resentful of the prosperity of this Black community. The district was rebuilt, but never reached the economic status it once attained.[3]

My parents explained to me that we were going back to Oklahoma to teach my grandparents, uncles, aunts, and other family members the word of the true gospel. Most of my father's family members obeyed the gospel, but only two of my mother's sisters obeyed. We set off for Tulsa. It was around 1941. Suffice it to say, I was excited to see what living in Tulsa was going to be like.

---

3   Smith, Jessie Carney. "Tulsa Oklahoma Race Riot (1921)." Freedom Facts and Firsts: 400 Years of the African American Civil Rights Experience, by Jessica Carney Smith and Linda T. Wynn, 1st ed., Visible Ink Press, 2009. Credo Reference.

We found a widow lady living alone in a big house who opened her home to us. She lived close to my new school, Carver Junior High. Almost as soon as we got settled into our new home, we began looking for a church family. After being there for about five or six weeks, my dad met a gentleman who he told that he had not located a Church of Christ. The man repeated the name, thinking out loud, "Church of Christ…Church of Christ… you know, I think there's a little group of people down on King Street near the park in an elderly lady's living room. I think that's what they call themselves." Well, the next Sunday we went to the place the man told my dad about. We found the house and learned that this was the Church of Christ. The whole church consisted of eight people, all women except one sister who had a 14-year-old son. They were so happy to see us and they immediately welcomed us to the family. They were really glad to meet my dad and to have someone to help the young man with leading prayer in service and other responsibilities during the week. They had a visiting minister come to preach on Sundays from nearby cities such as Oklahoma City, Muskogee, and sometimes even Okmulgee too.

It didn't take long for my family and me to settle into our new life in Tulsa and to bond with our new church family.

***

Growing up I had no plans to go to college and one day I shared this sentiment with my mom. She immediately responded.

"Yes, you are going to college. Not only that, you are going to a Christian College," she said.

"I am?"

"Yes, you are." Well, mom said it, so I believed it.

One Sunday we were enjoying our Sunday service and listening to the visiting minister's sermon. About halfway through his sermon he said, "You young people (all two of us), don't even think about marrying outside of the church." I'm sure there was a whole bunch more he said after that, but I couldn't tell you what it was. All I know is that I heard that statement and did not hear any more of that sermon. I could hardly wait to talk to my dad.

When we got in the car, I told my dad, "We have a serious problem." My dad asked me what our problem was and I said, "Did you hear what the preacher said about we young people not marrying out of the church? Do you see the problem? We young people are two of us. I do not have a choice. There's only one boy here."

My dad said, "Well, we can't have a gospel meeting in this sister's house."

"I guess we have to have an outdoor meeting. You know how when we were baptized we were outside under a tent? I guess we better try to have an outdoor gospel meeting," I said.

My dad said, "I will look into it," and that was that.

He searched for a lot on a nice street in the city. He found one right on the main Black street in Tulsa in the Greenwood neighborhood on Greenwood Avenue. He got some men to help him build some benches so the meeting attendees would have somewhere to sit. They made a platform for the preacher, got a loudspeaker, a good preacher, and we were ready to have our open-air meeting.

The first night we had people standing on the sidewalk listening. One of those listeners was Mr. Pitts who went home and told his wife about the good bible preaching. The Pitts family was a nice Black family that didn't live too far from us. I hadn't met them yet, but I knew of them. Mrs. Pitts was interested in what was being preached and came the next night. She became a little angry because of the truth of the word, but my mom and dad went over to her and thanked her for coming and asked her if she would let them come to her home to study the bible with her. She agreed to that and soon after, she was baptized. Mr. Pitts was baptized later, but unfortunately he did not live quite a year afterwards. He died of tuberculosis. I was 14 years old at the time and I read the obituary at the funeral. We did not have a church building yet so we used a Baptist church building for the funeral.

When I met Mrs. Pitts I learned that she had six boys and one girl. I said to myself, "Praise the Lord, maybe I can get one of her boys!" I learned that her sons Carroll, Joe, and Dorris attended Booker T. Washington High School, my same school. I didn't know what they looked like yet so when I went to school, I asked my classmates, "Do you know the Pitts boys?"

"Yes," they said.

"Well, I need to meet them."

They pointed out Joe C. Pitts to me. Joe was in the ninth grade and I was in the 10th, so he was too young for me. Then they pointed out an older Pitts boy at the school, Dorris. He looked pretty good, but he was my height. I wanted my husband to be a head above me, so that wasn't going to work either. My friends shared with me that Carroll, the oldest brother, had been drafted into the Navy right out of high school. It was then that I decided I'd wait to meet Carroll.

I had learned from Bro. Hogan's Christian Echo[4] that we faithful Christians should write to our Christian servicemen. I decided that this would be a good thing for me to do. Bro. Hogan had the addresses in the Echo. I chose four or five of them to correspond with. In the meantime, Carroll came home on his first furlough. I saw Carroll and said, "Yes, he is the one!" He was older than me, taller than me, and very handsome. I got acquainted with Carroll early on. I told him that I was writing Christian servicemen. I asked

---

4   Established by Minister G. P. Bowser in 1902, The Christian Echo is the oldest periodical in continued publication representing African American Churches of Christ. R. N. Hogan served as its second editor in 1953.

him if he would like for me to put his name on my list. He quickly said he would love to hear from me. We began corresponding and we were enjoying the letters from each other. In fact, his letters got to be so nice, I gave up on writing to the other servicemen and concentrated on Carroll's letters. Soon enough his letters became dating material. We kept writing and planning for us to be together forever. I told him that I would be going to Pepperdine College in Los Angeles when I graduated from high school. He decided that he would like to go to Pepperdine too! By the time he came home for the second furlough, we were fully dating.

Chapter 3

California, Here I Come

My mom had me get what information I needed from Pepperdine to apply for admission as she prepared to send me to L.A. once I graduated from high school. It was 1945, just before the end of the War. She sent me in May, but before I left, I wrote to my good friend Catherine in Phoenix letting her know I would be going to L.A. Cat wrote me back saying that she would like to go with me to L.A, but she had one more week of school. She asked me to come to her house and wait until she finished her last week of school and she would go with me. So I did. I did not share that bit of news with my mom of course. I knew she would have a fit. My mom did not believe in playing around. She'd rather me go straight to L.A. and get ready for school as planned.

I left and traveled to Cat's house. I decided to take the bus for the trip. I had a nice one week visit with her family and then Cat and I traveled to L.A. on the train. We did not know where we would stay because Cat had not had time to contact any of her relatives and I didn't know anybody there.

Well, fortunately by the time we got there, we had figured it out. After we arrived in L.A. we got a cab to take us to an aunt of Catherine's who lived in Watts. Her house was small and it was made like one of the houses I had lived in in Oklahoma. You may know the ones I mean, where you sort of just walk straight through. I think they call it a shotgun style. Unfortunately, once we arrived, we learned that the aunt did not have room for us to stay there. So Catherine decided we should go to Long Beach where she had an uncle. There was a room for us at her uncle's house, which was great news to me because after all that traveling, I was about ready to sleep anywhere I could find a safe and comfortable bed. We settled in and enjoyed our summer visit with Catherine's family, but as the end of summer approached, Catherine had to go back home because she had her senior year to do. So when the summer was over, she went back and left me with her relatives.

Soon after Catherine left, I decided I was not staying in L.A. or going to Pepperdine. There were so many people in L.A. Just being out there by myself was a lot. I wasn't used to big churches and it seemed like the people in them weren't too friendly to me. I was ready to go back to Oklahoma. I did not want to tell my mom that I did not register for Pepperdine. I hadn't even gone out there. I was too ashamed to tell her and I did not want to ask her to send me a ticket to come home. So I decided to work and make my fare back. In retrospect, if I had written to my father, he probably would have sent my fare and maybe not even told my mother. I don't know, but I knew my mother would be disappointed the most.

I got a job working at a drugstore. In my day, there were drugstores that had lunch counters. They sold sandwiches, ice cream, pop, etc. At first, I worked as a dishwasher and then at the front counter working the fountain. I ate the food they made there. I was living in Long Beach and traveling to L.A. each day on the big Red Car[5] to work. I worked about two months to make my fare and went home carrying an additional 15 pounds from eating what I was serving.

---

5   Red Car was the nickname for the Pacific Electric Railway Company mass transit system in L.A. which used electrically powered streetcars.

When I reached home in Oklahoma, my mother was shocked and confused.

"Bernice, why are you here? Aren't you in school?"

"No, Mom. I'm standing here in front of you."

She wanted to know what happened. I told her that I did not want to stay in L.A. because the people there were not friendly.

"Ok. Now you just sit down and write Pepperdine to find out when the next entrance date is. We are going to take you out there and enroll you," she said.

Like I said, my mother didn't play around.

I obeyed her command and received an answer that I could enter in January 1946.

Mom said, "We'll prepare to take you back to California in December, get you registered into Pepperdine, and return back to Oklahoma."

My mom was set on that being the plan and dad and I followed right behind her. However, like life goes sometimes, things did not quite work out that way.

Chapter 4

A New Home

In the 1940s, California experienced a major influx of Blacks from the South and Mid-Western regions of the country. This westward movement is known as the Second Great Migration. From 1940 to 1946, the Black population in Los Angeles more than doubled from 63,774 to 133,082. Los Angeles had the largest population of Blacks in California. The Second World War brought an immediate need for workers in the defense industry. By the summer of 1942, defense companies who previously barred Blacks from skilled work employment began to drop racial restrictions.[6]

Like many other cities in the U.S., Blacks were confined to living in a segregated section of the city with few exceptions. In Los Angeles, that area was restricted to Central Avenue and eastward of that street. With the rise in population, the area became overcrowded while Whites in surrounding neighborhoods continued to uphold restrictive real estate covenants to keep Blacks from moving into their neighborhoods. It wasn't until 1948 that these restrictions became legally unenforceable as deemed in the landmark Supreme Court case Shelley v. Kraemer.

---

6   DeGraaf, Lawrence. *Negro Migration to Los Angeles, 1930-1950.* Dissertation, UCLA,1962.

My parents got a senior man to stay in our house to look after it while they were gone. They told him that they would probably be gone about two weeks while taking me to Los Angeles to attend Pepperdine College. My parents' plan was just to help me move to Los Angeles to get settled before starting my first semester at Pepperdine.

We left sometime in December 1945 headed to sunny California in our dependable 1936 Chevy. We stopped in Flagstaff, Arizona and I remember it was snowing. My dad was both scared to go and scared to stop. We didn't know what to do, but he decided to keep on driving. When we got to L.A. we discovered that the city was really crowded. It was 1945. The War was just over and soldiers were returning home to restart their lives. Like many other large cities across the nation, there was a housing shortage. Dad couldn't find a place to stay. Fortunately, he remembered he had a friend that had left Oklahoma and came to L.A. He had his phone number so we got in touch with him. He and his family had an extra room that they rented to my parents. I don't remember where I stayed.

A few days after we arrived, my dad's friend took my parents to his job site on a whim. Next thing you know, both of my parents had been hired after being in L.A. for only three days! They just loved it out here. The weather was beautiful and they were so quickly employed, they decided to stay for a while. They especially loved that Bro. Cassius was in L.A.. Bro. Cassius was the minister that came to Tulsa and built us a church building. Oh my parents just loved him! He was a minister at Compton Avenue Church of Christ in Los Angeles. That's where my parents decided to worship. Later, my dad became an elder at Compton Avenue too. So much for a trip just to move me into college!

After a couple of weeks, my mother started writing to her sisters in Oklahoma letting them know that she and my father would not be back because they got jobs in L.A. My mom told my aunt to sell certain items in the house. "We'll be back as soon as we get a break from our job. We'll come back and sell the house," she said.

Meanwhile, I started attending classes at Pepperdine College. Now at that time, Blacks could attend college, but they did not let Blacks stay in the dormitories on campus. However, I was able to stay with one of the teachers who lived on Pepperdine's property, Mrs. Finn, her husband, and their daughter. I think I did light housework and watched the little girl when Mrs. Finn wasn't there.

Carroll and I were still dating through the mail and making life plans. Carroll learned some things about Pepperdine and decided he would like to attend a Christian college too. Pepperdine was the only Church of Christ affiliated college that would enroll Black students. There were about five or six Blacks there when I entered.

Carroll was discharged from the Navy in 1946 and he got in touch with Pepperdine to get the information he needed for him to enroll. He came out to L.A. to get ready. I had gone to summer school to catch up with my class, the one I should have graduated with had I entered in September 1945. Carroll enrolled on his GI bill, but he did not attend long because one day when I came home from school, I told my mom that Carroll and I want to get married.

"Married!" she shouted. Then she thought about it for a few seconds, and finally she said, "Married or not, you're finishing school." I had two years to go, but I thought I was grown and smart enough to be a student and a wife at the same time. Wrong! After we thought about it, Carroll and I decided that he would drop out of Pepperdine and get a job and wait until I finished. Then he would re-enter.

Well we got married on Easter Sunday, April of 1947. Bro. Cassius did the wedding ceremony for Carroll and me. We were married at the church at 43rd and McKinley Avenue. That was before Figueroa Church of Christ was established where Carroll would later preach. I told Bro. Cassius I wanted him to do the ceremony, but I didn't want to use the Compton Avenue church for my wedding where I was a member and he was the minister because I wanted to walk down a center aisle. The church building at Compton Avenue didn't have a center aisle, you had to go along the side.

I had two or three high school classmates as bridesmaids, along with Cat who came in from Phoenix as my maid of honor. She had gotten married earlier that same year. Dad was late getting to the church because he was picking up someone at the bus or train station. He had me all upset. People told me, "Don't get upset. You'll have to fix your face." I prayed to God for a nice wedding and it was. It was a beautiful ceremony.

Carroll and I enjoyed being married. He was very romantic. We often went to the park and engaged in playful activities like practicing acrobatic moves and exercising. Our favorite park to go to was the one close to Compton Avenue and 103rd Street.

Though I requested them as a child, my mother would never buy me skates. I wanted to learn how to skate, but she wouldn't let me because she had this friend who had a kid who broke her arm or something or another. So she wouldn't let me skate. When I got married, Carroll bought me a pair! You know I didn't need to be learning how to skate at that time, but he would take me over to that park to try to learn how to skate. I didn't do too well with that, but it didn't matter because I finally got a chance to learn after I got married. That was fun.

A few months into our marriage, Carroll found a job at the Firestone Tire and Rubber Company and was also able to help Bro. Cassius with the church work at Compton Avenue Church of Christ. I continued studying at Pepperdine.

At the beginning of our marriage we were living in a room in a rooming house. I began to dream of living in a house of our own. It was something I had thought about for years and unlike nowadays when women do all kinds of things on their own, back then, buying a house and living in it by myself was out of the question. Now that I was married, it was as good a time as any.

One day I was walking down the street and I saw this new little house for sale on 112th Street near Central Avenue. Brand new, never lived in. "That would be good for Carroll and me," I thought. "Let me find my dad and see if he will lend me the down payment." I knew my dad was resourceful, so I started with him.

I found my dad and said, "I was walking down the street and I saw this cute little house for sale…brand new, never lived in and Carroll and I would like to have it."

He said, "Well, what's stopping you?"

I said, "We need a down payment."

"How much is the down payment?"

"$850."

"Don't you have $850?"

"No, we don't have it."

"How much does the house cost?"

"$7,850."

My dad said he would check it out, which he did, and he decided he would lend us the money for the down payment. Now we had to have a discussion about my payback plan. I asked my Dad how much money I was to pay back monthly on my loan. He said, "a dollar a day," which would be $30 a month. I figured that was good because my mortgage payment was $50.24 a month. After we agreed on that plan, my dad told me that he's going to move in with us and live out his money, which he did. So he and my mom came. This arrangement worked out fine for the two years I had before graduation because my mom would help me with my housework and I could keep up with my lessons. When I subtracted the last $30 on my loan, I told my dad that next month, "Now you give me $30 for staying here." My dad said, "I'm moving. I have my house already. I was just waiting until I lived out my bill." I realized that he was just helping me be a wife and a student at the same time. After that, my parents moved out and I graduated.

Shortly after my graduation, Carroll quit his job with Firestone Rubber and Tire Company and re-entered Pepperdine College full time on his GI bill again. With a Business Secretarial degree in hand, I pursued jobs in the clerical field. My first job after graduation was with a L.A. City school library. I worked there for maybe two years, took a test, and got another job working at L.A. City College in a stenographic pool. There were six or eight of us and a supervisor. We were there to work for the teachers to type up their tests, letters, or whatever secretarial work they needed.

Evidently, Carroll had enjoyed what he was doing at Compton Avenue creating the bulletin and visiting and teaching classes because when he re-entered Pepperdine in 1949, he changed his major from Business Administration to Theology. When he attended Pepperdine the first time when I was still in school, his major was Business Administration and mine was Business Secretarial Science. I said that we'd work together well. But now, Lord have mercy! Now that he was changing his major, I didn't know what to do. I had decided from a child that I did not want to marry a minister. They moved around from one church to another and I wanted to stay in one place. I made up my mind that I did not want that kind of life. Every night our conversation in bed would go something like, "Change your major back to Business Administration." But then right after, I would think to myself, "No, I shouldn't be this selfish. I *want* this man to work for the Lord." I repented of that and I asked Carroll for forgiveness for not wanting him to work for the Lord. After that, I just prayed to the Lord to let me be the best minister's wife I could be. I asked Carroll to forgive me for not wanting him to be a preacher. Oh Lordy, but I can say that I *didn't* marry one. He *became* one while we were married. But you know, God worked it out because that's the only thing I hated about ministers, moving around, not staying in one place, and we didn't have to do that too much. The Lord just worked that out for me.

During this time, Carroll's baby sister, Wilma, finished high school in Oklahoma. She wanted to come out here to L.A. for a better life. So we sent for her and she came out and stayed with us. She got a job at General Hospital and worked and she took some classes at L.A. City College.

Some time later we were asked by Pepperdine to move into Normandie Village at 79th and Normandie Avenue on Pepperdine's campus where the married couples and families lived in dormitories. They wanted us to break the racial barrier for the college. There weren't any Blacks living on the campus period. They knew us, since Carroll taught Religion. So, we did it. We moved out there and rented out our house. Wilma came with us. We all lived in the Village until Carroll graduated from Pepperdine College in 1954.

Chapter 5

Stepping Out on Faith

Los Angeles and Oakland were not the only destinations for Blacks moving to California. As early as the 1880s, Blacks moved to Central California in Kern County. Farm work in California paid higher wages than what was offered in southern states and there was a shortage of laborers to work the labor-intensive crop of cotton. Many were recruited from the South for agricultural work by Kern County planters (formerly Southerners themselves) to work cotton, a new commodity in the area. With new economic opportunity came some of the vestiges of racial oppression from the South in the form of the Klu Klux Klan established in the 1920s in the county.[7] Despite this deterrent, Blacks in Kern County became an established demographic over the decades.

It didn't seem like Carroll was at Pepperdine long before it was time to move again. In 1955 after his graduation, Carroll was asked to come to Bakersfield, California for his ministry at the Baker Street Church of Christ. The church had a parsonage behind the church building for us to live in. I didn't care for living in a parson-

---

7   Roldan, Gary. *Activities of the Ku Klux Klan in Kern and Los Angeles Counties, California, During the 1920s.* MA Thesis, California State University, Fresno, 1996. pp. 41-42.

age, but I remembered what I had said years before about being the best minister's wife I could be, so I did my best to be cooperative and content. Bakersfield was not too far from L.A., just a little over 100 miles. My parents could come back and forth easily. But after a while, they bought a house in Bakersfield too.

It was 1955 and we did not have any kids. We had been married since 1947. We had a home, a means of income, and each other, but we also wanted children. It was at this point that we decided to adopt. We started the process of filling out lots of paperwork and being interviewed by the Los Angeles County Bureau of Adoptions, but had to start it over again with the equivalent department in Kern County. I did not try for a full time job while in Bakersfield. I did not want to be working a full time, permanent job when I was waiting for an adoption opportunity.

On my last assignment with L.A. City College, I was assigned to this librarian. She had requested me and she loved me to death the first time I went. She kept requesting me. I didn't like going to her because she just talked, talked, and talked some more. One day, after hours of her dictating to me and going on and on, as we're leaving, I told her that my husband and I are moving to Bakersfield. She was so sad to hear that. "Oh, I sure hate to lose you, but I have a librarian friend in Bakersfield. I'm going to write him and tell him about you 'cause I would like for him to have you." As she's telling me this I'm thinking to myself, "Bakerfield is prejudiced…I've been there," but I let her go on.

After I got the house together and Carroll and I had been in Bakersfield for a couple of months, I said to myself, "Maybe I'll go see this man my former supervisor in L.A. told me about." I found out how to get to the library in Bakersfield and went out there. When I arrived, I went up to the counter and told the lady who I was and who I was there to see. She called the man and said, "Somebody out here wants to see you." When the man came out the door and saw me, he turned red. He came on over to the counter and I told him who I was. He said, "Oh yes, I did receive notification, but you know that position was just filled." How convenient. I thanked him and left. I should have told him what I was thinking, but I didn't.

Before leaving L.A., I had taken a civil service test to get on a list of qualified candidates for government employment so I could work in Bakersfield. After two or three months there, I was called for jobs, but I never got chosen when sent for the interview. The employer could interview three people and make a choice, but it was never me until one day, a secretary working at the Highway Patrol wanted to take a three-week vacation, but her boss said she had to get a replacement for her job before she could leave. She called the Department of Employment to inquire of someone willing to work only three weeks, but to no avail. Those people wanted regular jobs. Finally, this secretary called the Employment Office again and she was told about Mrs. Pitts who only wanted a part time job because she was waiting on the adoption of children. The lady called me in for an interview and she liked my appearance and my intelligence and personality. She hired me. The employers liked me too. In fact, when the three weeks were over, they wanted to give me a permanent job, which I refused because of the adoption coming up; but after that short stint, the secretary from the State Highway Patrol told all of her friends to request Mrs. Pitts to relieve them when they wanted to take their vacation. I was requested in all different state and county offices in Bakersfield. I became a permanent, part time worker and got vacation pay and sick leave. People would see me in those different offices, not just *notice* me, but *see* me. They would say amongst themselves, "I saw that lady at so and so…and then I saw her somewhere else. What does she do?"

Wherever I'm working, I usually enjoy what I'm doing. Even if I don't, I do the best job I can. I found that that's the best attitude you can have when facing blatant racism…a positive attitude and persistence.

Eventually Carroll and I received word from the state's adoption service. In 1956, we got our first child, Philip, when he was 14 months old. We were so excited and he brought us so much joy. Philip was a very quiet baby, though he was already talking when we got him. We wanted another child and about a year later, God blessed us with our second adopted child, Pamela, at 10 months old. I was excited that Pamela was still wearing diapers because I didn't get to go through that stage with Philip. Pamela was a busy baby. She was into everything, opening all of the kitchen cabinets and getting into anything she could find. As she got older, she was the grown one, always protecting Philip as if he were the baby of the family. They were about three years apart in age.

I had started going on walks in the neighborhood ever since we got settled into Bakersfield. I was going down the street one day and I saw this house for sale. It was on T Street. It had two bedrooms and a den, perfect for a growing family. I think we had stayed in the parsonage a couple of years at that point and I was ready to go. I knew that if we left, the church could use the parsonage for bible classes, which would have been great because the church had grown so much that they had outgrown the church building itself. We were using the parsonage for classes while we were also living there. Carroll would not let me fry bacon on Sunday morning because we would be having classes in the kitchen area and in the living room and he didn't want the smell of bacon in the air. So when I saw this house in Bakersfield, I had to go see my dad again. Dad was generous enough to loan Carroll and me money to buy our first house, I hoped that he would assist us again.

"Dad, I need the equity out of the house in L.A. so I can pay down on a house I like in Bakersfield."

"You give me the first little house I bought for you on 112th Street and take the equity out of it and then you can buy over there," he said.

So that's what we did. The deal went through with the Bakersfield house and we moved into our new home. I don't know how long my dad kept our house in L.A. I can't remember. All I know is that we bought that house in Bakersfield and I was a whole lot happier.

Carroll and I were enjoying our family. I remember when Philip reached age 5. I enrolled him in kindergarten. He did not want to go at first, but he later got used to it. Before the school year was over, Philip got a new teacher and came home excited to tell me the news. I asked him, "Is she a Negro?" He thought about it for a few moments and said, "I don't know. I'll ask her tomorrow." I quickly said, "No, don't ask her. I will go meet her later."

***

One day after about six or seven years in Bakersfield, I saw Bro. Hogan and Bro. Bowers get out of a car in front of the house. They likely had just come from a meeting because a visiting minister was with them, Bro. K. K. Mitchell from Alabama. At this point we had been in Bakersfield for several years already and never had house visits from the local preachers. When I saw these three preachers coming up my sidewalk, I told Carroll, "Now if they're coming here to ask you to go to Texas or anywhere out of California, the answer is no." When they came in I offered them water, or whatever juice we had in the refrigerator, and then I went on back to whatever I was doing. I was going crazy waiting for them to leave. What did they want? What did they need to talk to Carroll about?

Finally after some time, Carroll called me back into the room and said, "They're getting ready to leave. Come on back and tell them goodbye." I came back in and told them goodbye, but I was going crazy wanting to know what they said. As they left the house and headed back to the car, I said to Carroll, "What did they want?"

"Let them get in the car first."

When they left down the street, Carroll said, "They want me to come back to L.A. and be the third minister at Figueroa. I'm going to the bedroom to pray about this matter."

I said, "Well while you're praying, I will be packing," I laughed. "I know God is going to answer your prayer. So, you do the praying and I'll start packing." He went on in the room.

When he came back out he said, "Well I decided that it will be a good thing to do." He let the brothers know that he would take the work. He would come back to L.A. to work with Bro. Hogan at Figueroa.

As for our house in Bakersfield, the men got in touch with movers and the movers handled the rest. I mean, it was the easiest move we ever made. The week we were supposed to be leaving, people were coming to the house to say goodbye and they couldn't believe I was leaving that week and hadn't packed one box. Well, the movers told me I didn't have to do anything. I believed them so I didn't do a thing. They came and packed everything up and labeled it. Then when they brought it down to L.A., they put everything in the kitchen exactly where it belonged. It was incredible.

Once the actual move was taken care of, there was another thing we had to do. Before, Carroll and I had used the equity in the first house we bought on 112th Street to purchase the Bakersfield house. Now we needed the equity from the Bakersfield house to buy again in L.A. Once again, my dad took care of the situation. Carroll and I took time to search for another house in L.A. to buy. We checked out some places for sale with realtors and found a good deal on two houses on a lot on Van Buren Avenue, close to Washington High School. We thought that would be a good thing so we took that deal. My dad gave us the equity out of the Bakersfield house for us to purchase the house on Van Buren. Carroll, the kids, and I moved into the front house and my parents moved into the back house. My mother could walk out her front door across her lawn and into my back door. We were pretty cozy and we all got settled into our new situation.

Bernice Maxine Carr as a toddler

The Pitts Family: From left to right - Carroll Jr., Olander (in back of Carroll), Carroll Sr., Dorris, Joe (in lap), Algertha, Opie. Wilma and Clarence were not born yet.

Carroll Pitts Jr. in the Navy, 1943

Wedding Day, April 6, 1947
We were wed at 43rd and McKinley Church of Christ.

Bernice in her bridal gown

Fun at the park at 103rd and Compton Avenue during the early years of our marriage.

Graduation from Pepperdine College, 1949

My parents, Mack and Lena Carr, attended Carroll's graduation from Pepperdine College in 1954. My parents loved Carroll as if he were their son.

Carroll's graduation from Pepperdine College, 1954

At the invitation of Pepperdine College in 1953, we moved into Normandie Village, Pepperdine's dormitory for married couples, to break the race barrier.

Pepperdine Senior College Photos

Bernice in 1949

Carroll in 1954

Pepperdine Alumni Dinners c. 1950

Bernice joins the workforce, 1950

Bernice poses with co-workers at Los Angeles City College, 1955

Dorris, Carroll and Joe all served as ministers in California.

Carroll and his brother Dorris, 1955

Baker Street Church of Christ, Bakersfield, California, 1955

Phillip and Bernice, 1960

Pitts Family Christmas photo, 1966

Chapter 6

Establishing New Roots

After the Shelley v. Kraemer Supreme Court decision in 1948, Blacks, who could afford to do so, began to move westward and northward from the segregated Central Avenue community into other neighborhoods in Los Angeles. They desired to live in safe, uncrowded neighborhoods to raise their families.[8] Many White homeowners, spurred by fears of declining property values and integration of children in local schools, began to sell their homes and move to the suburbs. Other homeowners used tactics to keep Black families out of their neighborhoods. This included purchasing homes for sale by neighbors to keep Blacks from moving into the neighborhood, bombings, vandalism, threats of violence and cross burnings on the lawns of newly purchased homes by Blacks.[9] Despite these aggressions, the Black population increased in once predominantly White neighborhoods. Churches in these neighborhoods were left with the decision to remain within a neighborhood, disband, or follow their White congregants to the suburbs.[10]

---

8   Sides, Josh. *L.A. City Limits: African American Los Angeles from the Great Depression to the Present*. University of California Press, 2003, p. 95.
9   U.S. Commission on Civil Rights, Hearings, p. 159.
10 Mulder, Mark T. *Shades of White Flight: Evangelical Congregations and Urban Departure*. Rutgers University Press, 2015.

It was 1962 and we were adjusting nicely to our new life back in L.A. At this point Pamela was old enough to attend school and the kids settled well into their routines. We were requested to come back to L.A. to work with Bros. Hogan and Bowers at Figueroa Church of Christ, but this turned out to be short lived. Southwest Church of Christ, a White congregation located at Normandie Avenue and 64th Street, was planning to sell their building. The brothers (mostly my husband, I think) asked them not to remove the Church of Christ out of this growing Black community. A few conversations and some signed paperwork later, three other congregations came together to purchase the Southwest building and renamed it Normandie Church of Christ. The church was re-established in August 1963 and my husband became the first minister. It began with 33 members from other congregations. Carroll worked very hard to grow the church and it grew very fast. He encouraged the new members to live a Christian life and to teach others.

My experience as a minister's wife while in Bakersfield was very helpful for my work with Carroll's new congregation. In the beginning, the few of us members worked together to get everything going regarding the building from the cleaning to preparing the building for worship. All of the work was done voluntarily. I was the first church secretary until we were able to afford one. However my role as secretary continued until Carroll left this world because I continued to be his secretary at home.

We were a happy, loving congregation. We had great times with all of our different ministries. We had song groups, visitation teams, children's programs, and chorus groups from elementary through high school. I remember the good times we had with the visitation teams vividly. We had four teams: 1, 2, 3, and 4, and each team worked one week of the month visiting members. We went in pairs and we received points for the number of member visits we made. I think we went by quarters every three months to count up points. The team with the most points at the end of the quarter was honored by not having to work at all while the other three teams planned a dinner. They bought the food and the winning team fellowshipped and ate. Sometimes when my partners and I would go for our visit we would find no one at home. That meant we would not get any points with that particular visit. So I would think about someone else who we could visit so that we could earn our points. It was nice, friendly competition that kept our church family connected.

On Saturday we had children's meetings and gatherings of different groups. I remember one Saturday I brought my children to the church building for the Saturday children activities and I dropped them off and told them I would pick them up later. I was going to pick up something at Sears located on Vermont and Slauson. On my return, I decided to pass Gage off of Vermont and go to 64th Street instead. When I drove to Budlong, I saw a "House for Sale by Owner" sign posted in the front yard. Mind you, we had not lived in the current house we had just moved into from Bakersfield for long. However, I couldn't help but to stop my car, walk to the porch, and ring the doorbell. A man came to the door and I said, "Excuse me Sir, but I see that you have a 'For Sale By Owner' sign in your yard. Would it be possible for me to see the house now?"

"Yes, ma'am," he said in a Caribbean accent.

He was probably from one of the Islands. He had the accent and dark complexion. He opened the door for me to come in and I said, "Oh before I come in, do you have two baths?" He said, "Yes, ma'am, two baths." I came in and walked through the house. I liked the floorplan, but when I was about to leave the man informed me that the one-bedroom apartment over the double garage next door also came with the house. I was really shocked and happy to learn that information because I knew that having that apartment would help pay my mortgage should I be able to buy the house.

I'm sure you can guess what happened next. I went to my dad to tell him about the deal. My dad checked it out and he decided to help me buy the house. So once again, we put our house on the market. At this time my mom had a nephew who lived in Perris, California who had promised her a lot if my parents would build a house on it and live on it. My mother was happy about that because she loved raising baby chicks and country living. Her house was being built, but it wasn't ready yet, so our move was perfect timing. Our home was sold and the place we were buying was ready for us to move into. We all moved into the house on Budlong since my parents' house was not ready yet. We made the move, but it was not nearly as seamless as the last one. This time we had so many boxes and it took several trips to get it all to the new house, but eventually we did it. About six weeks later my parents' house was ready. They moved out, which created room for the whole family. My dad told me that that would be the last time he would help me buy a house. That was fine with me. I am in the same house to this day.

***

One day I drove home from work, pulled into the driveway, and opened the garage door. I did not see our boxes we had stored in the garage. They were not there. When I saw Carroll I asked him what happened to all our boxes that were in the garage. He said he put them out on the curb because we had been there a year and no one had gone out to the garage to get anything yet. After I recovered from the initial shock of our boxed belongings no longer being there, I thought to myself, he's right. So I dismissed it from my mind. For most couples, this may have been a point of dissension. After having been married for a while, I understood this wasn't a big deal. I didn't like to fuss. We loved our new home and my parents loved their new home, so everyone was happy, and that was all that mattered.

After returning back to L.A. from Bakersfield, I got a part time job at the junior high school on 92nd and Hoover. As the kids got older and started attending school, I had more time on my hands. The children were now young adolescents. Pamela was very outgoing and personable and she loved being with other children, teens, and young adults. She was very intelligent, insightful, and energetic. If you just watched her and listened to her talk, you would see that she was bubbly, likable, and genuine in her conversations with her contemporaries. Phil was more of an introvert, cool, composed, and behind the scenes. He was athletic, a bodybuilder, and a trendsetter in appearance and style. Though I worked part time off and on when the kids were younger, I realized that I still didn't want to take a regular job because I wanted to be able to travel with Carroll when he went places for work. If he had to travel for work, I was going to be right there with him. My parents would step in to watch the kids while we were gone.

While at the junior high school, I worked in the principal's office as a steno clerk. While there I met three other clerks and we became good friends. All of us were college grads and should have had better paying jobs. So the three of us returned to college to take a couple of classes in order to get teaching credentials. After that, I got on the list for substitute teaching. I liked this method of teaching. It was nice being a substitute teacher because I was able to travel with my husband when he was requested for meetings, lectureships, etc. I was used to meeting a lot of ministers when they came to meetings, but you never meet their wives. I didn't meet Sis. Hogan until I moved to Los Angeles. The ministers' wives didn't travel, but I was going to travel with my husband. I only had to inform the sub desk that I would be unavailable for a certain period of time and that's what made it so special for me. I was well known and was requested mostly from high school business teachers because my field was secretarial science. It seemed like I was working more than the regular teachers were! The teachers would just take off knowing that there was a substitute teacher available. They would call me first and say, "I have requested you so if the people call you, you already know." That worked out well. I stayed on the sub list for 14 years.

I worked at George Washington Preparatory High School in Los Angeles. At that time, George McKenna was principal[11]. I started working there as a substitute teacher. Mr. McKenna told his faculty that "anybody who wants to be off, request Mrs. Pitts. We will put her where we want her when she gets here." I was at Washington almost every day. If it wasn't one teacher it was another that had me there. Then finally, Mr. McKenna talked me into taking a three-hour a day assignment working in the counseling office. I enjoyed that better than the idea of teaching. I didn't really want to teach. So I took the job in the counseling office and did that for a while. But eventually I told Mr. McKenna that I was not happy with this three-hour a day thing. I said, "I come out here, get involved with the counseling job, and then the three hours are up and I have to stop in the middle and go home."

"Well Mrs. Pitts, what would you like to do?" I said, "I would like to work three full days and the next week two." Well he agreed

---

11   Dr. George J. McKenna III became principal at George Washington High School (later George Washington Preparatory High School) in 1979. At that time, the high school was known for gangs, drug dealing, and gun violence. Under his direction, McKenna reformed the school from a failing institution to a high school where 80% of its graduates were accepted into college. Denzel Washington played the role of McKenna in the major motion picture *The George McKenna Story* in 1986.

and that's what I did. That schedule was really nice. I could finally get something finished. I would work three days this week and two days the next week and if something was coming up in my personal life, I would work the whole week. He just let me do it the way I wanted to do it. It was lovely. I was now working two to three times a week in the schools, raising teenagers, and heavily involved in church activities like teaching classes, visiting the sick, and singing in nursing homes weekly. Sometimes I worked five days one week and skipped the next week because I was attending a lectureship or something else and needed the days off.

Life was beautiful, including my marriage. There were times when Carroll would still write a love letter to me although we lived in the same house. This was throughout our entire marriage. I would write letters to him too. Carroll was so busy with his church stuff that I used to get really sad because he would spend so much time working and I would feel lonely. So I would write him a letter, even mail it in the mail too. I would explain to him how I needed more attention. Sometimes I would make reservations at a hotel or something for us. I would call my mother and tell her I would need her to come babysit my kids because I needed to take Carroll somewhere so I could be with him. My mother would come down from Perris and she would stay with the kids. Maybe sometimes I just wanted to stay with him and we would just go to dinner or something. We did that for years. We continued to date each other. My mother would stay with the kids and we would go to dinner and I would call my mother later and tell her that we were going to stay overnight. My parents were very supportive. By me being an only child my parents were glad to do it. I have to laugh when I say this, they just wanted me to be happy, truly, and I will always love them for that. They were crazy about Carroll, the son they didn't have of their own.

Chapter 7

Journeys to New Lands

The McCurchins

Alfred McCurchin came to the states from Guyana in 1964 to study Automotive Technology. He attended the National (Technical) School on Figueroa and Santa Barbara Boulevard (now Martin Luther King, Jr. Boulevard). Gloria, his wife, came a few months later. When Bro. McCurchin finished in 1965 he was on a student visa and not ready to go back home to Guyana. He found Pepperdine College and started attending there in 1966. He was told about Carroll and went to Normandie to meet him. He was baptized that same year.

Carroll asked Bro. McCurchin to attend Sunset School of Preaching and serve as a missionary in his home country of Guyana. Bro. McCurchin agreed and Normandie paid for his tuition and two years later, he went on a preliminary mission trip to Guyana in 1968 during a summer break from school. Carroll and I visited Guyana on that trip in 1968. People were so friendly. There were very few cars on the road. Everyone was walking. While we were there we had vacation bible school in the day and gospel meetings at night. I loved teaching the kids vacation bible school songs. They especially loved, "If You're Happy and You Know It."

The church sat above an apartment in a two-story building, so when the kids stomped their feet, it was so loud! We had a good time with that. At this point in time, there were no Churches of Christ in Guyana.

Bro. McCurchin graduated from Sunset in June 1969. He, Gloria, and their young son Mervyn, who was 5 years old at the time, moved back to Guyana in 1969 to establish a congregation. The church was started in a rented house on Laluni Street in Demerara, Georgetown. Ten people from Normandie visited the new church including us, Rose Allison, Melvin Herndon, and Tony Stafford. Other missionaries from the States came for a period of time. The women would stay at the McCurchin house and the men would stay in bedrooms in the church building. The church grew to over 100 members at one point. Churches of Christ began to spread over the country. At least 60 congregations were started between 1969 and 1978. People were groomed by the missionaries to take over the church. Mervyn learned how to bring the message and would lead singing. Angie, their daughter, began teaching at 5 years old. I went to Guyana with Carroll on every trip except when he stayed for a month. I would sing, knock on doors, greet and talk with people, teach bible class and read poems. My brother-in-law, Dorris Pitts and others came to Guyana in 1971 to assist with a church in the Cuarantine area while my brother-in-law Joe worked with a mission group in Trinidad.

The McCurchins lived there from 1969 to 1978. Bro. McCurchin came back to the states in 1978 and the remainder of the family moved back in 1981.

Bro. Eno Otoyo and Mission Work in Nigeria

I don't remember anymore how we met Bro. Eno Otoyo. I don't know if someone from here went to Nigeria on missionary work and met him while introducing him to the gospel or not, but I know we met him while he solicited support for the work of the church in his home country. The Normandie congregation gave a lot of support to the missionary work there and took charge of the collection of funds of other congregations across the brotherhood. We became really close with Otoyo, especially after he met his future wife, LaVera, here in the states. When they got married, we were living in Bakersfield. They decided that they wanted to come to Bakersfield for their honeymoon, and they didn't go to a hotel either *(laughter)*! They spent their honeymoon at our house right there with us.

Carroll and I enjoyed visiting them in Nigeria in 1978. There were a number of congregations established in many villages in the Oron Clan of Akwa Ibom State, Nigeria. Carroll preached while I taught bible classes and sang. The missionary work there contributed to the establishment of a multipurpose assembly hall on the campus of the Christian Secondary Tech School. There were separate bath and shower facilities for boys and girls, a Mission Guest House for visitors to the campus, a medical center, and a mini-farm designed to train people in drip irrigation. Carroll brought small trees with him to Nigeria for Otoyo to plant at that farm. They bear fruit to this day.

Holy Land Trips (Late 1970s - Early 1980s)

Carroll and I always wanted to go to the Holy Land, but we didn't want to go just by ourselves. We wanted to go with a group. One day I was looking at a newsletter subscription and I came across a cruise advertisement. I said, "Carroll this is our chance to go to the Holy Land. I'm going to get in touch with the hosts and see what we need to do." So I did. They said the tour group would be leaving from Dallas, Texas. From there we would take a chartered plane to the Holy Land and board the cruise ship. A few days later, Carroll and I were signed up and getting prepared to go.[12]

There were about 400 people on the plane and we sang during the flight. Oh, that was the best trip. It was a long plane ride too. We probably flew about 4 or 5 hours before we started to get sleepy; the singing soon turned into snores. I remember sleeping on the plane and feeling the sun on me as we flew into the daytime. It was the strangest feeling. When we arrived the guides had buses to pick us up. Supposedly the guides thought they were going to do some touring, but the people were falling out of their seats with sleep. They said, "We may as well take them on over to the ship. They won't see anything if we tour now." So they took us over to the ship so we could go to bed.

Once we were all rested we were ready to explore the land. Oh, I was so excited. The history told to us by the tour hosts felt like attending a bible class. They told us about ancient places and biblical people, stories I'd heard about all my life. It reminded me of reading the bible. It was so exciting. I could hardly wait to get back to L.A. to tell my church people about this place.

One night we were at dinner with the captain of the ship and we were so excited to just be there. I said to Carroll, "I can hardly wait to get back home to tell the others about this place." The captain heard me talking about this to my husband and said, "Why don't you and your husband become tour hosts?"

I asked, "What do we have to do?"

He said, "Just what you said you're going to do when you get back. That's what you do. Get people to come on the trip. Then you and your husband come back with your people for free."

---

12 Trips to the Holy Land were organized by Fowler Tours, a Christian-based tour agency in Dallas, Texas.

I said, "Oh really? How many people do we have to have?"

He said, "You need six apiece."

I said, "Oh my goodness, I'll have those before I get back home." He told us what we were to do and that's what we did. I was the one doing all the organizing stuff, but Carroll was one of the people in charge of the bus. They had about 8 buses to take us around the Holy Land for the tour. Carroll's job was to keep track of who's on his bus and be sure everyone was all on and checked in.

I had 18 people with me that first year we took people over there, Carroll and I only needed 12 for us to go for free. So I think they gave me $100 a piece to spend on the trip for those extra people. Everybody that we took with us was so excited, like I was on my first trip. By the second trip I was noticing things I hadn't seen or noticed before. I said, "Did I see this last time? I don't remember seeing this before." It was truly amazing. We went to the cities of Corinth and Ephesus and Mount of Olives to walk where Jesus walked, ride on the sea of Galilee, and witness where they hung Jesus, Golgotha. I could hardly contain myself to be in all those places.

I was never a picture taker, but when we were going to Israel, I took pictures. I bought Carroll one of those Instamatic cameras. Carroll would take picture after picture, but when he got back home, you didn't know what was what. In our photo album I have little notes written under mine so we could at least tell the places we went.

We did that four times over four years. Carroll did it five times because that fifth time, a group went in June and July. Carroll and I had both gone in June and I wasn't up for turning right back around and going again. I couldn't do it, it was just too much traveling. It took me too long to get over jet lag and the time difference. So I sat that trip out.

I think my faith in God and His promises has brought me through so many things that I just had the faith that He was going to bring me through it all. And He has all these years.

Chapter 8

Loss of Loved Ones

Loss of Pamela (1975)

I lost my daughter on November 14th, 1975. Losing Pamela, I think, was the worst thing for me to go through. Philip, Pamela, and their friend Teri Pressley were driving to a friend's house when they were hit by an oncoming car. Philip and Teri were hurt, but Pamela did not make it.

At one point I thought I was going to have to move from our house because I would drive past the corner every day where it happened. It is just a block up from the house. I could hardly get across the street without breaking down in tears. But God is good. He knows what you're going through and He helped me to finally get to the point where I could drive down the street without crying. Pamela gave birth to our first grandson, Jerrai Brown, just two years before she passed. Carroll and I focused on raising him. I had to stay involved with all the things that I was doing before the accident. I couldn't give up anything because I knew if I stopped, I wouldn't be able to get back into it. So I kept going, and of course my church family was so supportive.

Loss of Carroll (1987)

When I lost my husband, God got me through that too. Carroll and I had talked about everything, even death. I have this little story that we had been talking about death and I told him, "If I go first from this world, you better mourn for me for at least a year." I said, "I would say two, but I don't want to press it, because men marry quickly after the woman dies. So, I wouldn't say two years, but at least a year." He just laughed about that. He didn't say anything about if he went first. If he had, I would have told him that I wouldn't be remarrying again. I said one marriage is enough for me. I've been a widow for 36 years. This year, 2023, it's been 36 years.

Carroll was diagnosed with cancer in 1987. By us talking all the time about everything together, he told me he didn't want to go to the hospital. He didn't want to die in a hospital. He wanted to die at home. I prayed to the Lord when he did get sick, "Please don't let him get down, I don't know anything about caretaking a person." He honored that request for me. He didn't let him stay a long time in his suffering.

Carroll kept going until the end. The Churches of Christ in Los Angeles were having that month-long tent meeting out in Carson. We went every night. That was in August of 1987. He died in September 1987. He was getting tired of driving the freeway out there every night, so I did the driving. I didn't want to drive on the freeway at night, but I did and I complained about it every night too. He decided he was going to help me drive on the freeway. One particular night when the meeting was over, I came out of the tent and went out to the car. I would meet Carroll at the car because he would always leave early. He didn't want to be in the crowd with cancer. This time he's sitting under the steering wheel.

I said, "What are you doing?"

He said, "I'm going to show you how easy it is to do this trip."

I let him. We got in the car and he drove on down to Avalon. "You see how easy it is? You just drive on down to Avalon and stay in this lane." He's telling me everything. "You get on the freeway and be sure to stay in the right lane because if you stay over there, you're going to end up in San Pedro." So he stayed in the right lane and went on. "You see how easy it is?" Be sure you do this and be sure you do that. He did this until the last night of the meeting.

About two weeks before he died, Bertha Mae Love agreed to come stay with us. I think she was a retired registered nurse. We had a hospital bed and a twin bed in the same room. She moved in here with us. She used the twin bed in the room with him. I was still working at Washington High School part time.

Bro. Ernest Shaw, who was also a preacher, was sick at the same time as Carroll. Bro. Shaw died two weeks earlier than Carroll. One day I told Carroll, "I'm going to stop on the way from work and attend the funeral for Bro. Shaw at the Vermont Avenue Church."

He said, "I want to go."

I said, "You can't go to the funeral. I'm going to work before the funeral so you can't go to the funeral."

But he would have gone if I let him. I stopped by the funeral. I told Carroll that, "I'll be back. I'm just going to be gone for three hours." So, he accepted that he couldn't go. But anyway, when he was passing, I was sitting in that chair in the den in there and Bertha Mae Love said, "I think you better go lay down in the bed so you can get better rest and I'll wake you up if necessary." I went on and got in my bed. Then early the next morning she woke me up, maybe around 4:00 in the morning. "I think it's time for you to come in now." Carroll was passing. I went in and just held his hand until he took his last breath. There were people at the house, church members here when it happened. Later when they were getting ready to leave the house, I said, "Oh excuse me everybody, before you go. I have two tickets for the Southwestern Christian College Dinner Day and I need somebody to take me."

Everyone in the room was quiet.

Iva Voldase said, "Sis. Pitts, I'll take you."

"It's on Sunday, you know." We were having two services at Normandie at that time. I said, "We'll go to the 8 o'clock early service and then we'll go to the luncheon in San Bernardino."

She agreed with me. The next morning, I got up and got ready for church. I entered Normandie and people were shocked to death to see me. "Sis. Pitts! How could you…? You just lost your husband yesterday. How could you be here?"

I said, "I sure didn't want to be home. This is where I should be! Getting all this attention, love, and encouragement." I said, "That's why I'm here, not there, cause why would I want to stay at home and cry?"

After all the questioning and answering, Iva and I drove to San Bernardino and found the hotel where the luncheon was being served. I opened the banquet room door to go in and at that same time somebody was announcing that Bro. Pitts passed last night. I opened the door and the people were so shocked to see me. They acted like they didn't know what to do with me. They came down and got me from the door and took me up to the head table. I'm thinking, "What is wrong with these people?" So, we went on. We got through the luncheon and then I told Iva, "We won't be able to get back to Normandie for the 6 o'clock church. Would you mind if we stayed out here for worship?"

She said, "Well, yeah we could. I would have to call my son and let him know I'm down here so he'll know I'll be late coming home."

She did that and then I asked somebody standing close to me, "Excuse me. Do you know where the closest Church of Christ is to this hotel?"

The person said, "I think 11th St. Church of Christ, but I don't think they have a 6 o'clock church. I think they meet at 7."

I said, "Oh no, we can't wait until 7."

She said, "Well I think Riverside Church of Christ meets at 6."

I said, "Can somebody direct her (Iva) how to go from here to that church?"

Somebody did and we went on over to that church for 6 o'clock service. The same thing happened. I opened the door to go in and somebody was announcing about Bro. Pitts. Then he said, "…and Sis. Pitts is walking in." We went on in and stayed for their service and I had everybody so shocked. Then we drove back home.

I guess I was in shock when I was doing it all. I don't know what it was, but it got me through that day. I didn't stop doing anything that Carroll and I did together. I kept right on going with church activities and taking cruises. I was the one that got it all together, got the people to go and all that. I just kept right on doing it. We kept right on having fun. I think if you don't do it the way I did it, you would end up letting the grief take your life away.

I think I have been an example to people who do lose their mate or experience some other terrible loss. Some of them have talked to me about it. I have had people, years ago, call me and say that somebody had lost their child and they gave them my name to call. So it is nice to know that me keeping on was helpful to somebody.

Chapter 9

Keep on Living

In 1992 Washington High wanted to transfer me from working in the counselor's office and put me back in the classroom which I definitely did not wish to do. They said if I did not take this job, I would have to retire or just quit. So I decided to retire that day. I was 66 years old.

For my 75th birthday we did a cruise all the way from Mexico to Hawaii. It was so nice. I'm always so tired when I take these trips. I'm tired when I leave home from all the preparation and tired when I come home after the trip, but it was really nice to cruise. It took five days to get there. I just rested and ate and went to the movies. I think there were 11 friends on that trip. We cruised at night and toured different islands during the day. It was so nice. On my 80th birthday, I had a big luncheon at the Proud Bird; had about 200 people there. Then on my 85th birthday I went on a California coastal cruise. I didn't even know they had that until I was checking into it to see what I wanted to do to celebrate. I chose to take that cruise and my agenda said that our first stop would be San Francisco. We were set to leave L.A. on Saturday evening. When they told me our first stop would be San Francisco on Sunday morning, I called the Metropolitan Church of Christ in San Francisco where Bro. Kinwood Devore was the minister to let them know I was celebrating my 85th birthday. I told them we (I had 15 with me on this trip) were on a cruise and that our first stop was San Francisco, so since it would be Sunday, we would like to worship with them. But we can't do the morning worship because we weren't set to get there until 1 o'clock in the afternoon on the ship so we would like to worship at the 6 o'clock service. Whoever I was talking to was so excited.

"Oh, that would be so nice."

I said, "Well, I have people with me so you'll need to bring maybe a couple of vans down to the ship to pick us up. We will do the 6 o'clock service."

They were so excited to hear that we were coming. Bro. Devore came down to pick us up from the port that Sunday afternoon with his van along with one of the elders of the church in a second van. They took us to worship at their congregation. I think I had more members with me than they did. I think I had 15 and they had 12 or 13. But this preacher, that I didn't know, he really preached like he had 3,000 people in there. After service, one of the brothers took a picture of my group. The group that was in Kinwood Devore's van, after the worship was over, he took them all over downtown San Francisco. I told him later, I'm glad I wasn't on your van because I sure didn't want to be touring. I just wanted to get back to the ship, but the group that was on that van really enjoyed it.

For my 90th birthday we took a trip to Alaska. That was a gift. The Alaska trip was a cruise and land trip. We had a 3-day land part. After the cruise we got on a bus and they took us to our first destination. There was a steward on the bus. I said to him, "Excuse me sir, we are a group of Christians who are on this trip together and when we get together as a group we like to know where the people are from that are on the trip with us." I said, "We like to sing and we like to find out what state the people are from that's with us."

The man looked puzzled. He said, "How would you do that?"

I said, "Well I would get up and walk down the aisle and ask the people what states they are from and write them down. Then I use an 'Amen' chorus to sing to them and they would raise their hands or something when I call the state."

He said, "Oh, ok."

I did what I needed to do. I asked the passengers what states they were from and found out there were 32 states represented on that bus. Then I went back to the front of the bus and told them what we were going to do, then led the bus in song. They really enjoyed it.

All the trips that I take, I get involved with the passengers if it's allowed. One time, I was taking a group of sisters to Arizona's Ladies Day in Phoenix. It was just going to be that Saturday. I got the people together who wanted to go. I think there were 32 of us. We all dressed pretty because we didn't have to take anything with us. When we got to the airport, I remember standing in line to board the plane and the stewardess said, "Oh, nice pretty ladies dressed so pretty. Where are you going?"

"Oh, we're a group of Christian ladies going to Phoenix for a Ladies Day in Phoenix," I said.

"Does this group sing?"

I said, "Oh yes. We're not a singing group, but we sing when we are together."

She said, "Well, when we get aboard, would you like to sing?"

"Yes, we'd love to sing."

She asked me, which was really nice. I usually had to ask myself.

When we got on the plane and took off and got way up in the sky, the stewardess came on the PA system and let the travelers know that there are a group of ladies who want to sing a song for us, a group of Christian ladies. She came back and sat on the arm of somebody's seat to listen. Everyone enjoyed it.

Shortly after that, I did the same thing on the train. Sis. Taylor McKenzie in San Diego called me one day and said she had been asked to speak at the Church of Christ in Portland. She said, "I'm getting a group of sisters to come from here and I want you to get a group to come from there in L.A. We're going on Amtrak."

I said, "Amtrak? We'll drive and meet you guys there."

"No, Sis. Pitts. You can't do that. We need you on the train because you know how to entertain us and entertain the people too."

"Ok," I said.

She said, "You get the sisters, as many as you can, there."

I think we had about 15 in that group too. She got her group there and I got a group here. Then they got their train there and came up here and then they had to change and get on the train that we were getting on. After we rode quite a while, the conductor came walking through. "Excuse me sir, but we are a group of Christian ladies. We're going to a ladies' session in Portland. When we get together like this in a group, we like to sing. Can we sing on this train?"

He looked around as if to show me that we were not the only ones in the car. He kind of leaned down to me and said, "Why don't you start singing softly and then just get a little louder, and then if nobody objects, go 'head on."

And that's what we did. And of course, as usual, the people enjoyed it. Then after a while, the people in our car were going down the train and telling the people up there about the singers. Later on, the conductor came back through and said, "The people are enjoying the singing, so we would like for the whole train to hear. All of you can't go down there to the next car, but can I ask about half of you, about 7 or 8 to go where the PA is and sing so the whole train can hear?"

So we did. Half of us went. After that, the people started coming back requesting songs, like we were a paid group. That was so much fun. Then when we got to Portland, we were so tired and sleepy (it was an overnight ride on the train and we didn't have a car with beds). We didn't have much time because the meeting was going to start soon. We had to hurry up and get to the hotel and get ourselves together. Finally, we got to the church. We were waiting for the program to get started, but nothing was happening. I said, "This group is going to fall out on the floor asleep if we don't get started soon. What's happening?"

They said, "Well we're waiting for our song leader."

"Oh, honey. That's not a problem. I'll be the song leader."

That went well. After the program was over, we boarded our bus and headed back to the train station. When we started to get on the train, the people that work on the train said, "Oh here come the singers." Now as you can imagine, we were worn out by then, but the train workers had been telling the passengers, "Just wait 'til the singers come." When we got on the train the train started moving and the people started asking, "When are the singers going to start?" I said, "We're very, very tired and sleepy. I know the ladies are going to have to get some sleep before we get to L.A." One man said, "Well I'm getting off in Santa Barbara. Could you all sing before we get there?" So we ended up doing some singing coming back, but not as much as we did going because the ladies were tired and sleepy. But I don't mind asking. They can only say no.

Chapter 10

Life Now - What's Next

One morning when I arrived at Sis. Pitts' house with my P-95 mask secured tightly on my face, she greeted me with this sentence, "I changed my mind about writing my book."
"What?" I said.
"There are so many church families in my life whose stories I want to include in my life story. There are so many gone, but I'm listing some that are still living. I have a whole list here that are still living." She proceeded to list the names of about 25 women. "I think they would enjoy being in the book. I would enjoy, if I am still living, I would enjoy reading their stories."

It was October 15th, 2021 and we were still in the throes of the COVID-19 pandemic. A number of longtime members from Normandie and other congregations had unexpectedly passed away over the last year and a half. Some families held funeral services in church parking lots while other deaths were mourned in isolation without ceremony.

I breathed a sigh of relief that she wanted to continue writing the book. She just wanted to document and honor the lives of friends who were still a part of her life. After further discussion, we realized that including so many stories would change the perspective and purpose of the book. We continued on the trajectory of her telling the narrative of her life from her point of view.

Loss of Philip

In 2009, I lost my son Philip to cancer. He was 54 years old. It was a sad and difficult service to plan. At the age of 13, Philip was baptized into Christ. He enjoyed working with the youth in all different programs. He graduated from the high school I worked at, Washington High. After graduation from high school, Philip gave us our first grandchild and only granddaughter, Shanecia Pitts in 1972. Shanecia's grandmother, Bea Pressley, was a close and dear friend of mine. A few years later, Phil married our church secretary, Marlene Robinson and they had two boys, Michael and Delano Pitts.

***

God keeps blessing me to live all these years. Before the pandemic, I traveled regularly visiting friends or attending lectureships. I'm often requested to recite poems at different events. When I recite the poem "Heaven's Grocery Store," I move around because that kind of helps me to remember the words better. One time I did forget it. I was at a Crusade for Christ or something and we were having our Women's Day. They had about 350 to 400 women sitting in the audience. I told them that I wanted to recite a poem in memory of my play mom that I had out here that had died. They said, "Oh yes, we'd be glad to do that." When it was time for me to say my poem, I went to the stage, quoted a few verses and all of a sudden, the words just left. I didn't panic. I said, "We have around 300 sisters sitting out here in this audience. Don't one of you have this poem in your purse?" And somebody did! This sister got up and she came toward me with the poem.

She reached out to me and I said, "I don't have my glasses up here. I won't be able to read it." I said, "Please kind of look through and see if you can see about where I stopped. I think if you just give me one word I can get started again." She told me about where I was in the poem and I went on with it. After the meeting was over, some lady came up to me and said, "Was that a skit?"

I said, "No, it wasn't a skit."

She said, "You really forgot?"

"Yes."

She said, "You're so brave. I would have been crying and I just would have been so embarrassed."

I said, "I didn't have time to do all of that. I wanted to finish my poem."

I tried and stayed active doing what I enjoyed doing as best I could during the pandemic. I was very busy on Zoom programs. I met many sisters online and enrolled in two weekday, 8 am bible classes, which I enjoyed except for the early hour. I was really looking forward to returning to our building for worship. I missed our fellowship, the hugs, and kisses, and of course, the SINGING!

Chapter 11

Stepping Out Again

It is 2023 and COVID-19 restrictions have been lifted by California State Governor, Gavin Newsome. What better way to resume community gathering than to have a 95th birthday party for Sis. Pitts! The party took place in May at the Proud Bird, a large venue restaurant in Los Angeles. Over 100 of her closest friends and family members gathered to celebrate. Longtime friends Cat Bellamy and Iva Voldase, also in their 90s, were there to help celebrate the day with her. The program consisted of poetry reading, singing, and well wishers expressing their love for the nonagenarian. One long time friend and church member, Donald Harris, traveled all the way from Texas to share the day with her. He and Sis. Pitts stood at the podium together and shared that they had something in common. Both had learned to recite the alphabet backwards. Don noted that one day in kindergarten, his teacher said, "Donald Ray, say your ABC's." Wanting to impress his teacher and classmates, he started at the letter Z and made his way to A. His teacher promptly gave him a spanking, thinking Donald was sassing her! The audience roared with laughter. Sis. Pitts continued the presentation by singing her ABC's backwards! The audience was invited to sing along with her, but we couldn't catch up until she made it to "c, b, a."

After Don went back to his seat, Sis. Pitts walked in front of the podium toward her tables of guests, poised in a yellow suit. She began to recite the poem, "Heaven's Grocery Store." Without a microphone or notes, she strolled between the tables vividly reciting each line, pausing only for emphasis. It was a day to remember.

Pamela, Carroll, Jerrai, Bernice and Phillip, 1976

Our 35th Anniversary celebration at Normandie Church of Christ. We renewed our vows.

35th Anniversary - Bridal photo

35th Anniversary - The reception was in the church fellowship hall.

Bernice and Carroll meeting the captain at his reception dinner in 1979

Bernice Pitts in Egypt

Acropolis, Athens, Greece. Wilma, to the left of Carroll, came with us on this trip.

A trip with fellow Christians to Nigeria to visit the mission there under the guidance of the Otoyo Family, 1979

A newspaper clipping of Pamela's death

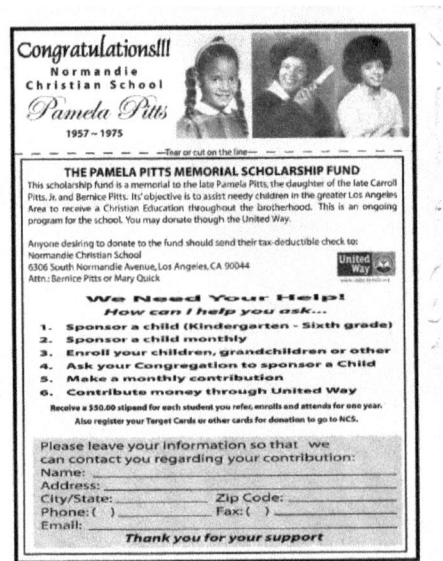

The ladies at Normandie created the Pamela Pitts Memorial Scholarship Fund soon after her passing.

Jerrai Brown, our grandson, was crowned King at the Normandie Christian School Annual Fundraiser.

Normandie Church of Christ honored Caroll with a banquet a few weeks before he passed away in October 1987.

Marlene, Phillip's wife and two sons, Michael and Delano

*Bernice Pitts at the 60th Anniversary Gala for
Normandie Church of Christ, 2023*

Epilogue

Written by Betty Lee

Bernice Pitts became an integral part of my life when I accepted Christ at the Normandie Church of Christ on February 14, 1976. I was baptized by the late Carroll Pitts, Jr. I have always honored the first lady of our congregation. She proudly exemplified the duties of the role she accepted when her husband became a minister. I smile when I think about MRSCPJ displayed on the license plate of her car to commemorate her continued loyalty to her late husband. I enjoy her optimistic outlook. She has a profound way of accentuating the positive and eliminating the negative in every aspect. She is a strong woman of God who makes no excuses for choices that she makes. Her hearty laughter and joyful spirit permeate any room.

We established a permanent bond when she began to refer to herself as my mom number 2. She has a fortress of daughters that she claims her position in our lives. I wear her claim as a badge of honor.

Bernice and I shared lunch on a Sunday afternoon in 2023, and her reflections were centered around her vision for the Normandie Christian School. She vowed that she would dedicate her time to the work that Carroll Pitts began in 1974 when the Normandie Christian School was established. Bernice shared flashbacks about her many fundraising efforts. The first being the queen and king coordination under the direction of the late school administrator, Mary Louise Quick. This was a major fundraising event for a few decades. Bernice chuckled as she remembered that her parents would ask her every year, "How much do we need to contribute for Jerrai (her grandson) to be crowned king?" She said whatever amount she projected and they would write the check. This project energized the students, the community, and sister congregations to step up contributions. The commitment involved work in organizing different fundraising activities such as selling candy or popcorn. The culmination was always displayed as a royal festivity.

Bernice then implemented the Pamela Pitts Scholarship fund as a memorial to her daughter. This program was designed to assist families with multiple children enrolled to offset tuition costs. The funds were also used to support underprivileged and at-risk students as well as high achievers by awarding scholarships. This fundraising project was easy for Bernice. She said that she did not work hard. She simply asked for donations and the church community responded.

Normandie Christian School held a luncheon annually as a fundraiser. The success of this event was apparent. The attendance has always been supported by all of the local congregations. Bernice worked tirelessly on ad solicitation. Her comment was that Bro. Pitts said she worked six months out of the year on that book. This fundraising campaign generated additional funds and at the same time, highlighted businesses within the church community.

Bernice introduced an elite program for members who wanted to support Christian education. She called it the $200 club. She sent letters and solicited from everyone on a personal basis. This program became an instant success.

I asked Bernice where this idea originated from. She remembered that Pepperdine University had a century club for $100 donations. She started at $200. She claimed that it was received with overwhelming response from members of the church community. The Normandie Christian School board members changed the program to the $300 club.

The next fundraiser that Bernice introduced was the Carroll Pitts Awards dinner, a fabulous black tie affair. Recognition focused on highlighting former students, their careers and achievements.

Bernice laughed and sighed saying, "I really did not realize how much was involved." She stated a few years ago that she finally decided that someone else should relieve her of the responsibilities associated with constantly reminding members to contribute and following up with thank you notes. So the Normandie Christian School Board of Directors took on the task.

When I asked Bernice what her vision for Normandie Christian School was today, her response was to rebuild attendance to pre-pandemic status. The Normandie Christian School is currently limited to pre-school enrollment.

Bernice resolved that she would like this book of reflections to be used as a fundraising tool for Normandie Christian School. She is hopeful that the school will sustain and the enrollment will rise again. This would be her legacy for Normandie Christian School which was established by her late husband almost five decades ago.

Her undeniable love for her husband transcended into the work that he loved…to keep Normandie Christian School solvent.

If you would like to make a donation to the Normandie Christian School, please visit: normandiechristian.org/donate. Thank you!

Love Letters from Carroll Pitts, Jr. to Bernice Maxine Pitts

MINISTERS
Carroll Pitts, Jr.
John B. Green, Jr.
Willard Crigler, Jr.

ELDERS
Carver Henderson
E. W. Singletary
Herman P. Thompson

CHURCH OF CHRIST
6306 S. NORMANDIE AVE./LOS ANGELES, CALIFORNIA 90044
PHONE 750-3212

DEACONS
Charles A. Ayers
Lawrence J. Clemons
Willie (Pete) Jackson
John W. Steen, Sr.
Benny J. Thomas, Sr.
Israel Twillie, Jr.

"IF IT CAN BE DONE, NORMANDIE CAN DO IT"

November 16, 1977

Mrs. Bernice Maxine Pitts
1154 W. 64th Street
Los Angeles, Calif., 90044

My Dearest Darling:

As I think back over the years of our married life, I feel that I am most blessed among preachers in our brotherhood. I have had a wonderful, understanding wife at my side, always encouraging me in whatever undertaking I have attempted to do.

You have been a good and cooperative wife in so many ways. And I know that this has not been easy for you, especially having to adjust to being a minister's wife and all that that implies. You have been understanding of my open and out-going personality to all, and even to the sisters in congregations all over our brotherhood. I know that you have had to struggle with that, which is what almost any wife would have to do. I must add, that in recent years and months you seem to be more adjusted to this touchy situation.

Accordingly, my love for you is even greater. I really enjoy being with you and being near you - the nearer the better - if you know what I mean!!! You are my sweetheart, my lover, my woman, my sex partner and my all in all. I still consider you my bride, my little girl and honestly and sincerely enjoy being married to you. In fact, I cannot conceive of myself not being married to you.

May our love for each other never wane, but may it continue to grow with the passing of time. I still enjoy your sweet kisses, the feel of your body near me in bed and just holding you when we embrace. I love you for being you, for putting up with me - which is saying quite a lot - and for being a good mother to our children and now to our grandson.

Keep loving me as I keep loving you, because I'm hopelessly hooked on you for the rest of my life, and I have absolutely no complaints.

A.M.L.   A.T.T.   Carroll

THE CHURCHES OF CHRIST SALUTE YOU. ROMANS 16:16

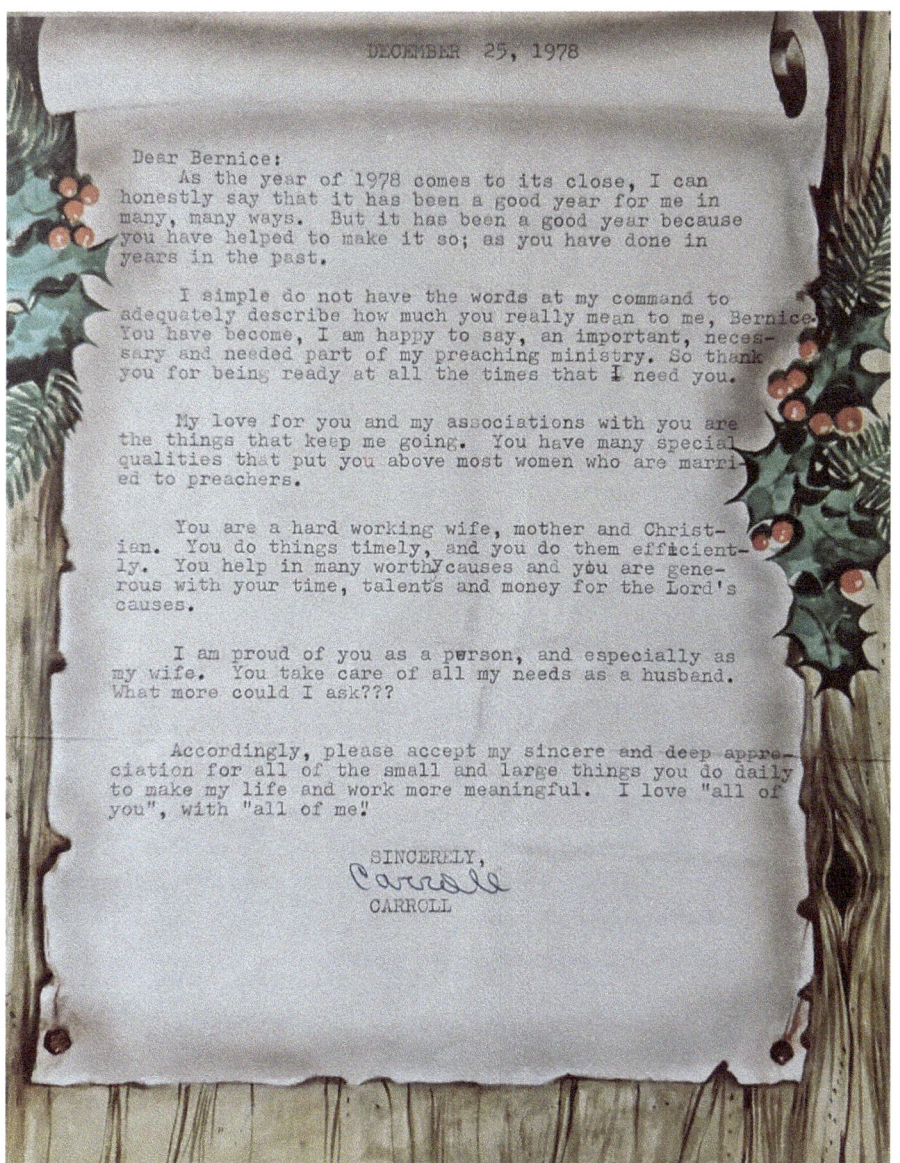

DECEMBER 25, 1978

Dear Bernice:

As the year of 1978 comes to its close, I can honestly say that it has been a good year for me in many, many ways. But it has been a good year because you have helped to make it so; as you have done in years in the past.

I simple do not have the words at my command to adequately describe how much you really mean to me, Bernice. You have become, I am happy to say, an important, necessary and needed part of my preaching ministry. So thank you for being ready at all the times that I need you.

My love for you and my associations with you are the things that keep me going. You have many special qualities that put you above most women who are married to preachers.

You are a hard working wife, mother and Christian. You do things timely, and you do them efficiently. You help in many worthy causes and you are generous with your time, talents and money for the Lord's causes.

I am proud of you as a person, and especially as my wife. You take care of all my needs as a husband. What more could I ask???

Accordingly, please accept my sincere and deep appreciation for all of the small and large things you do daily to make my life and work more meaningful. I love "all of you", with "all of me."

SINCERELY,

Carroll

CARROLL

MINISTERS
Carroll Pitts, Jr.
John B. Green, Jr.
Willard Crigler, Jr.

ELDERS
Carver Henderson
E. W. Singletary
Herman P. Thompson

CHURCH OF CHRIST
6306 S. NORMANDIE AVE./LOS ANGELES, CALIFORNIA 90044
PHONE 750-3212

DEACONS
Leonard Brooks
Lawrence J. Cle
James Collins
John W. Steen,
Benny J. Thomas
Israel Twillie, Jr.

"IF IT CAN BE DONE, NORMANDIE CAN DO IT"

TO MRS. BERNICE M. PITTS
ON
MOTHER'S DAY, 1979

Dear Bernice:

    Instead of buying you a printed Mother's Day Card, I have decided to express my feelings and deep appreciations for you in this short letter.

    First, I love you for just being "you". You are a unique person as far as I am concerned, and being married to you has been a source of joy and inspiration to me. You have served faithfully at my side through my 22 years as a gospel minister. Some of those years were not easy for us, as you well know. But I believe we have had more good years than bad ones.

    It takes a special woman to make a good minister's wife, because the job is so demanding on one's private and public life. I thank God that He gave me a sweet teen-age wife some 32 years ago whose name was Bernice Maxine Carr, who has grown and developed into an excellent mate for me. I am extreemely blessed, Bernice, to be married to you!!

    So on this Mother's Day, May 13, 1979, may you feel loved, respected, wanted and needed by me and Jerrai. To us you are "THE MOTHER" in the city of Los Angeles.

                                  AML   ATT

                                    Carroll Pitts, Jr.

MINISTERS
Carroll Pitts, Jr.
John B. Green, Jr.
Willard Crigler, Jr.

ELDERS
Carver Henderson
E. W. Singletary
Herman P. Thompson

CHURCH OF CHRIST
6306 S. NORMANDIE AVE./LOS ANGELES, CALIFORNIA 90044
PHONE 750-3212

DEACONS
Leonard Brooks
Lawrence J. Clemons
James Collins
John W. Steen, Sr.
Benny J. Thomas, Sr.
Israel Twillie, Jr.

"IF IT CAN BE DONE, NORMANDIE CAN DO IT"

March 10, 1980

Dear Bernice:

I am writing this letter to express my sincere and deep appreciation to you for the many wonderful, necessary and sometimes difficult contributions you make to our marriage. You play beautifully your roles as:
    a beautiful dedicated wife,
        an efficient home-maker,
            a loving mother to Jerrai,
                a financial provider to the family.

You also spend much extra time in the Lord's work in such areas as: Bible class teacher, lecturer for workshops and seminars, teaching home Bible classes, singing in the Adult Chorus, writing notes and sending cards to members, working as an officer and fund-raiser for the NCS CAPTAF, buying gifts for graduates, married couples, etc., working on Visitation and Zone programs and doing fund-raising for LACE and SwCC.

You are to be especially commended for all of the time and effort you put into the luncheons for Normandie Christian School and Southwestern in Terrell, TX. Your involvement in these two activities now runs for about ten (10) months out of each year.

Along with the above involvements you attend faithfully all services and special meetings at Normandie, you also attend functions often at other congregations, then too you spend much time doing what you call "a woman's functions", on such things as shopping, washing & ironing clothes, and keeping our home clean.

You, Bernice, are a beautiful, talented and dedicated person and wife. I love you very, very much, even more now than I did when we said 'I do' on the Easter Sunday afternoon in 1947 at the 43rd & McKinly Ave. Church of Christ before Bro. A. L. Cassius.

I thank God continually for putting us together as husband & wife. You have made my life happy and meaningful in so many ways. I can never say enough "words" to thank you for being the kind of wife, friend and lover you have been to me. ALL MY LOVE, ALL THE TIME.
        Your Grateful Husband
        Carroll

THE CHURCHES OF CHRIST SALUTE YOU. ROMANS 16:16

MINISTERS
Carroll Pitts, Jr.
John B. Green, Jr.
Willard Crigler, Jr.

ELDERS
Carver Henderson
E. W. Singletary
Herman P. Thompson

CHURCH OF CHRIST
6306 S. NORMANDIE AVE./LOS ANGELES, CALIFORNIA 90044
PHONE 750-3212

DEACONS
Leonard Brooks
Lawrence J. Clemons
James Collins
John W. Steen, Sr.
Benny J. Thomas, Sr.
Israel Twillie, Jr.

"IF IT CAN BE DONE, NORMANDIE CAN DO IT"
April 27, 1982

Dear BERNICE:

You and I have just recently went through one of the most unique experiences of our life; the repeating of our marriage vows as we celebrated our 35th wedding anniversary. I fully agree with many people who said that it was indeed the most beautiful wedding they had ever seen.

While a lot of people did many things to make it such a wonderful wedding, YOU WERE THE KEY PERSON that made the whole experience so uniquely unique. You spent much time and hard work in getting the 33 people to go with us on the Caribbean Cruise. You did the same kind of work on our wedding plans; such as getting the personell, the printing, clothing, food arrangements, decorations, the singing groups and our special music.

So both the wedding and the cruise were just BEAUFIUL, WONDERFUL and REWARDING experiences, especially for me. And I enjoyed them both even more because you, my lovely and sweet "BRIDE", had well planned both of them.

Bernice, you mean so much to me in so many ways and I simply can't list all of them in this letter. I am so very happy that our God put us together about 40 years ago and finally united us in marriage 35 years ago. You have been a FANTASTIC and BEAUTIFUL wife for me. You have made so many important contributions to me as a person, as a minister of the gospel and as your husband.

Being married to you for 35 years has really been the MOST REWARDING EXPERIENCE in my entire life. You and I make a good team together and we have accomplished many good things for the Lord and his work. We have proved a blessing for the congregations at 9512 Compton, Baker and Butte, Figueroa and in many special ways at Normandie for some 19 years.

I do not have the kind of words in my vocabulary to fully express my true love for you, also my deep appreciation for you. I'm looking forward to our retirement so we can spend MORE TIME TOGETHER - both in and out of the bed! (smile) Thank you for encouraging me, for supporting me, for listening to me, for helping me in so many ways and most of all FOR LOVING ME for some 35 years. My life has been richly blessed because of you, my beautiful wife.

Your blessed husband,

Carroll Jr.

Carroll Jr.

THE CHURCHES OF CHRIST SALUTE YOU. ROMANS 16:16

MINISTERS
Carroll Pitts, Jr.
Willard Crigler, Jr.

ELDERS
E. W. Singletary
Herman P. Thompson

CHURCH OF CHRIST
6306 S. NORMANDIE AVE./LOS ANGELES, CALIFORNIA 90044
PHONE 750-3212

DEACONS
Lawrence J. Clamons
James Collins
Willie (Pete) Jackson
John W. Steen, Sr.
Benny J. Thomas, Sr.
Jerry Cooks
Hue Hollomon
Maurice Jones

January, 1985

"IF IT CAN BE DONE, NORMANDIE CAN DO IT"

DEAR BERNICE:

As I begin this letter it is now 6 minutes after mid-night. I've just returned from a meeting. I checked with you and you are sleep in the bed. I am writing this letter to express, "in black and white", some feelings I have on my heart regarding you as my lovely wife.

First, you are the most unique person in this world to me. My body, my mind and my spirit have been closer to you and longer with you than with any other persons I know, even including my parents. I am so happy that I made the wise decision to marry you some 37 years ago. I still call you "my Lovely Teenage Bride." You have blessed and helped me in so many ways during our wonderful marriage together.

Secondly, I want to express my real thanks to you for the special care and concern you have given to me since my surgery in April of 1984. You really did a good job as my "private nurse". My complete recovery was do primarily to our prayers, those of the congregation and the wonderful ways you fed me, disciplined me, loved me and gave me a lot of TLC.

While it may be "nice" and "popular" being married to a preacher, it is not "easy"; especially being married to that guy named CARROLL PITTS, JR. I apologize for spending so many hours in my home office when I should spend more time with you and Jerrai. Like other employers, I am suppose to be off my job when I'm at home at night; especially after meetings, home Bible classes, church services, etc. One of my goals for this New Year is to spend more time with you as we watch T.V., relax, talk, and play games.

I really appreciate how you and I work as a successful team for the Lord's work in so many ways. God has blessed us in many ways. And he has especially blessed me by giving you to me as my lovely, talented, dedicated and beautiful wife. Again, I really do appreciate your help to me since my memory deficit has gotten worse in the past few months. Without you, I would be in very serious trouble.

Bernice, it is always a real joy to see you, to touch you, to hug you, to kiss you and to be "around you in the bed". Get the point? (Smile). Yes, honey, you have been, and continue to be, a blessing to me in many, many ways. It is my prayer that God will bless us so we can continue our work for him as we help people in these ways; and areas: our church leadership families; all members; especially the sick, disabled and those in trouble; non-Christians who need home Bible classes; L.A. brotherhood Christians and others around the US.A. Finally, Bernice I really love you, need you, want you and will never give you up. Since you have helped me and put up with me for about 37 years, you have my deepest "sympathy" and "congratulations", in that order.
A.M.L. A.T.T.   Carroll Pitts, Jr. *Carroll*

THE CHURCHES OF CHRIST SALUTE YOU. ROMANS 16:16

CHURCH OF CHRIST
6306 S. NORMANDIE AVE./LOS ANGELES, CALIFORNIA 90044
PHONE 750-3212

May 21, 1985

"IF IT CAN BE DONE, NORMANDIE CAN DO IT"

Mrs. Bernice Maxine Pitts
1154 W. 64th Street
Los Angeles, CA 90044

Dear Bernice:

I am writing this "small" and "special" letter to a "small" and "special" person whose name is BERNICE MAXINE PITTS. Since this is May 21, 1985, you know you have had the name Bernice for 40 years; plus 10 years; plus 7 years. That adds up to 57 years since you discovered America and the world back on May 21, in 1928, in the great state of Oklahoma. "Have a happy birthday, then "have" many more. I say this not only because you deserve and will enjoy many more years, but also because I and others need you "many more years."

I am so glad that my parents decided to leave Little Rock, AR, move to Shawnee, OK, then two years later decided to move to Tulsa, OK. Had those decision not been made at the right time regarding the right place, I would not have met the right person who was in Jr. High school. At that time you were named BERNICE MAXINE CARR.

In all seriousness, Bernice, you have been a real joyous blessing to your parents, your children, your grandchildren, your co-workers, your fellow preacher's wives, and especially to me as my lovely wife for the past 38 years. While my parents made some decisions, and your parents made a decision to move from Phoenix, AR, to Tulsa, OK, in my mind, it was God that put us together to do much work for him.

In conclusion, again, have a HAPPY BIRTHDAY and continue to enjoy God's many blessings upon you. I am so happy that you have helped me and supported me during my 30 years as a minister of the gospel. I still "love you", "need you" and will "keep you", until death do us part. Lastly, I know you will enjoy your cake baked by my "favorite daughter-in-law", (smile) Marlene Pitts. While it is your gift, May I have some of it too? I want some because that "sweet" cake will remind me of my "sweet" wife.

AML
ATT

Carroll

P.S. Do you still want to cash that $1,000 check soon? (smile)

THE CHURCHES OF CHRIST SALUTE YOU, ROMANS 16:16

CONGRATULATIONS TO BERNICE M. PITTS

Congratulations on our 39th Annivedsary, which is today, April 6, 1986;
Thank God you have you have helped me throughout all these years to get things fixed.

It has been a joy being with you, Bernice, for 3 decades, plus nine years;
We have been a blessing to each other; even during the time of tears.

I am happy that after we met each other in Jr. High School, a few years later God put us together as a married team;
I'm so glad that the lovely Bernice Maxine Carr, was the answer to my hopes and dream.

Bernice, you have been a special blessing to me over the past 31 years that I have preached God's will;
Darling, because of your help, support and cooperation, I have been able to get high ~~of the Lord~~ oh God's hill.

Not only have you blessed me as a minister's wife, but you have blessed sisters all over other states;
This was done by the seminars, workshops, songs and poems that you gave to make them better mates.

You have really encouraged and supported the Normandie Christian School and the Normandie congregation;
That's why many children, parents and church members join me in giving you a great congradulation.

You have been a good example as a minister's wife, and many other wifes have followed you;
They knew it's not always easy been married to a preacher, but they felt that if you could do it, with God's help tehy could too.

Again, I thank God that he gave me a beautiful, talented, young lady named Bernice Maxine Carr as my wife,
Therefore, I am happy, thrilled, excited, and looking foward to having you for the rest of my life.

written ~~Submitted~~ by,

Carnell Pitts, Jr.

About the Joint Author

Linda M. Cooks is a native Angeleno with an interest in African American history and cultural heritage. Her career has included real estate appraisal, cultural resource management, and academic librarianship. She is dedicated to creating opportunities for the preservation of narrative histories.

www.ingramcontent.com/pod-product-compliance
Lightning Source LLC
Chambersburg PA
CBHW041811050526
R18248400001B/R182484PG44119CBX00001B/1